A Hard Way to Make
an Easy Living

A Hard Way to Make an Easy Living

Corky Decker

Order this book online at www.trafford.com
or email orders@trafford.com

Most Trafford titles are also available at major online book retailers.

A Hard Way to Make an Easy Living was originally written by hand during long days and nights at sea while
commercial fishing in Alaska. It became a collaborative effort by Corky Decker, the author, and his wife at
the time, Barbara Gimlin, who turned his memories and writing into a manuscript. Although now divorced,
Barbara continued to assist Corky in the final editing for a story they both believe needs to be told.

Original oil painting of cover art done by Alaskan artist and
former crewmember Bruce W. Nelson.

Printed in the United States of America.

ISBN: 978-1-4269-5482-5 (sc)
ISBN: 978-1-4269-5483-2 (hc)
ISBN: 978-1-4269-5481-8 (e)

Library of Congress Control Number: 2011900566

Trafford rev. 01/27/2011

 www.trafford.com

North America & international
toll-free: 1 888 232 4444 (USA & Canada)
phone: 250 383 6864 ♦ fax: 812 355 4082

This book is dedicated to the memory of Oral Burch who so long ago gave a brash young man from Maine a chance. I'll look for you on the wings of the Albatross old man. May you forever soar in peace.

AUTHOR'S NOTE

Think about this. How can throwing back a dead fish and in most cases a valuable food fish ever help the stocks, the fishery, or the fishing industry as a whole? We as commercial fishermen feed people. We are the farmers of the world's oceans. We give up a lot going to sea, but it is a sacrifice we choose to make. We either fish within the rules and guidelines, or we bend them. In my case I broke a law that I did not agree with or believe in. I can honestly say I did what almost everyone else out there does, but the difference is that I got caught.

What law did I break? In layman's terms, in Alaska the powerful International Pacific Halibut Commission states that halibut can only be sold if they are caught on hook and line (today you also need a Individual Fishing Quota permit), so if the fish is caught by say a trawl net, it must be returned to the sea—dead or alive. If this isn't bad enough on its own, the government places a quota on how many tons of these valuable fish boats can discard before the bycatch numbers are reached and the fishery is shut down. These numbers are very small and are split between the entire high horsepower groundfish fleet. The quota can be caught in the matter of days, leaving a huge chunk of the target species uncaught.

The bottom line is, one special interest group dictates how a different industry is managed. To protect its own interests and keep the price of halibut high, the Halibut Commission disregards the fish that they seek to protect and consequently forces bad fisheries management on other fisheries. They flat out have their heads in the sand.

In November 2003, I stood in front of a federal judge and told him I was guilty of ordering the pre-sorting of halibut onboard the factory trawler I captained, the *Rebecca Irene*. I told the National Marine Fisheries Service that the whole bloody fleet pre-sorts halibut, that the data the observers collect is biased at best, and that fishermen are forced by incredible front office pressure to fish outside the law if we expect to turn a profit and be able to survive in the industry.

Six months later the government handed the Rebecca Irene a $360,000 fine. In addition the boat lost two six-week periods on its fishing permit the following year, which meant the equivalent of an additional $2–3 million fine in lost fishing time. I'm out of the industry, blackballed for life from fishing in Alaska, my marriage ended, and I'm starting over a world away from my old life. Sadly, it's a conclusion to a way of life. I am not resentful or bitter. Perhaps it was something that had to happen and the twisted humor of Neptune chose me and I was meant to tell this story.

What follows is a mostly true story, although I've change the names of some people to either protect them or because I'm afraid of them. Some of these events took place fairly recently, and others long ago, living only in my memories as seen through the eyes of a skinny young boy fascinated by the lure of the sea.

This isn't a story just about breaking the law, but what led up to that moment—and the incredible journey along the way.

TABLE OF CONTENTS

ALASKA

I'll never forget my first sight of the snow-covered peaks surrounding the sprawling city of Anchorage as I stepped off a jet at Anchorage International Airport in 1985. A lady tried to direct me into the terminal as I stood glued to the bottom of the stairs of the plane, staring at the giant mountains in total awe. A man behind me mumbled something about the damn tourists arriving earlier every year. I snapped out of my daze and stumbled towards the open terminal door, only to find my little sister laughing at me.

J.B. was well into her second semester at Alaska Pacific University and just from looking at her I could tell living in Alaska agreed with her. She was always petite and pretty, but now she looked different. She radiated a sense of style that can only be described as Alaskan, in the best sense of the word.

As we walked to the baggage claim area she told me she had lined up a bunch of her fishing friends to meet me. That was great since I had no plan whatsoever. At the ripe age of twenty-two, my hope was to find a job fishing. I retrieved my two sea bags filled with fishing clothes and foul weather gear. My other possessions had been stuffed into my parents' garage in western Massachusetts when I announced I was heading to Alaska, much to their astonishment.

J.B. went to get her car and drove up in what seemed to me a very new Saab 900 Turbo. I couldn't believe it. How could a college gal afford a vehicle like that? She hopped out laughing and gave me a slap on the back that nearly took me off my feet. She told me she picked it up from a doctor who was leaving the state for only $5,000. Still, five grand is five grand.

When she told me she was making over $200 a day working as a waitress at Simon and Seafort's restaurant in downtown Anchorage, I began to briefly wonder about other unexplored employment opportunities.

On the way to her apartment near the college she drove like a maniac, telling me she had to get it out of her system before the tourists arrived. All I could think about as I tried to hold on was she had to be a hooker or something. No one makes $200 a day as a waitress.

Well, she did make that kind of money on an average shift. In 1985 Anchorage was booming with oil and fishing money and the economy was strong. Simon and Seafort's was and remains today one of the finest restaurants in the state.

That evening I met several of J.B.'s friends who fished different areas in the state. One was even a woman—something I had never encountered back East, where fishing was largely a male-dominated profession. I couldn't even grasp the idea of a woman on a boat. We sat around in a tiny apartment and drank beers as I listened to stories about Alaska and commercial fishing. I asked a million questions and was thrilled by it all. There was one guy who spent summers in Kodiak, and that island seemed to have a special draw. There was a halibut opening there the following week, which is where I decided to go.

I spent the next two days with J.B. driving around Anchorage. She took me to a little resort town thirty-five miles south called Girdwood, with the state's largest downhill ski area. Being an avid skier, I fell in love with this quaint little community nestled in a valley surrounded by huge mountains. It was mid-April and I had never seen so much snow.

Little did I realize at the time, I would later put down roots and make Girdwood my home throughout the 1990s.

Soon it was time to catch a plane to Kodiak and look for work. J.B. dropped me off at the airport with my sea bags, $500 in cash, and a one-way airplane ticket to Kodiak Island. Oh shit was I scared.

KODIAK, ALASKA

Bears, Boats, and Opportunity

The very first thing I remember about Kodiak Island was the giant stuffed Kodiak brown bear at the airport. I couldn't believe it was real and figured it had to be some kind of joke. Bears do not get that big. I stood in front of that bear for a long time until a man came up to me and said, "Someone took a brownie 'bout that size out near Kalsin Bay. Guess it was after a rancher's cattle."

I turned to him and said, "You mean that's a real bear?" The guy just looked at me for a minute, shook his head, and started to walk away. I chased him down. I needed to know where the hell Kalsin Bay was, because that was one place I wanted to avoid. Once again I must have had tourist stamped all over my forehead.

I collected my bags and ventured outside the small airport terminal six miles from town and looked for a cab. I asked the driver to take me to the cheapest place to stay that was close to the boat harbor, all the while keeping a sharp eye out for those damn big bears on the way into town. I was expecting to see one charge the taxi any minute and even asked the guy driving why he didn't have a gun.

I think he must have thought I was on drugs because he never said a word to me and just kept looking at me in his rearview mirror before dropping me off at the Star Motel. I secured a room for three nights and went for a walk on the fishing docks.

The first boat I noticed was the *Royal Baron*, an old 85-foot wooden trawler. It was the only dragger I could find. Later I learned all the draggers were in the Bering Sea participating in Joint Venture fishing with foreign boats for various kinds of bottomfish.

It seemed like all the other boats—longliners, seiners, and crabbers—were gearing up for a halibut opening in three days. I didn't talk to anyone that night but just walked up each finger dock, taking it all in. I went down to cannery row and ended up at the All Alaskan fish processing plant. The plant was built in an old Liberty ship hull and was the strangest thing I had ever seen. This was truly a fishing town and I was in my element.

I had a beer at the Mecca, a downtown bar, and then went over to the Kodiak Cafe for a sandwich before calling J.B. to tell her about the bears, boats, and that I'd start looking for a job first thing in the morning. By 8 p.m. I was back in my room for a good night's sleep.

My entire life since the age of six had built up to this moment. My career in fishing began early, as a young boy working for tips on sport fishing boats off the coast of Maine. By my twenties I was hooked permanently and had worked a number of different fisheries. The only way I had ever earned money was by fishing, mostly out of Ogunquit, Maine. A promising college career while playing hockey became history as I was pulled in a different direction. The sea calls to some and when it does, its grip is not to be underestimated. Once you experience the power, wonder, and mystery of the ocean, it becomes a giant magnet.

In Maine I spent checks as fast as I could make them, living from trip to trip. Something had to change. The stories from my little sister about bountiful fishing in Alaska had beckoned, and now here I was. I would not step back in Maine for more than ten years until April 1996, when my wife and nine-month-old daughter accompanied me on a trip to see my parents.

THE EARLY YEARS

Maine

My dad bought my first fishing pole when I was just out of diapers. We fished for yellow perch and pumpkin seeds (a type of pan fish) on a lake at Camp Howe, a summer camp in western Massachusetts. My dad said I was so fish crazed, bonkers, and nuts, that from the very first day I longed to go fishing all the time, with whatever staff member I could round up to take me. If I wasn't fishing, I kept busy by scaring the camp staff with snakes. Usually somebody found the time to take me fishing.

I remember the first time my dad took me deep sea fishing at the age of five. The excitement I felt was like Christmas morning. I woke my mom and dad up at 5 a.m., even though we weren't due to meet the lobsterman who was taking us out until 8. My dad and I met the lobsterman at a small dock in Wells, Maine, where our family spent the summers. We met another father and son who were also going. Dad was seasick before we were outside the breakwater, but I was all over that boat. I had my head in every lobster pot, enchanted at the treasures. We caught pollock and cod all day and I completely forgot my poor, sick dad. I even went as far as peeing over his head while he laid in the forepeak resting near the toilet.

"Dad, hurry up, I gotta pee," I said, as I stepped on his hand and relieved myself.

That day became my fondest childhood memory. On the way home I looked my Dad in the eye and proudly told him I was going to be a fisherman, a sea captain. Being a high school teacher, and a seasick one at that, I'm not quite sure what he thought. But from that day forward I knew in my heart where I was going. During family walks at Wells Beach I would often hang behind and daydream of the day I would be at sea on my own boat.

The next summer our family was back living in Wells and I became a morning fixture at the docks of Perkins Cove. I finally convinced an old man named Al Voorhis to take me party fishing on his charter boat and agreed to work for tips as a deckhand. This was a great arrangement for both of us that lasted the next four summers. I got to spend my summers on the water and Al had free help.

Those early years were great. I learned knots, a little bit about how to read a compass and paper machine echo sounder, and met some great people who truly cared about me and made the days special. As a young boy, this gave me a special confidence not found in your normal playgrounds.

My early morning chores onboard the 46-foot *Marion*, an old wooden mine sweeper, included getting the rods, reels, and bait ready for the customers. The bait consisted of deep sea clams from frozen gallon tins that were thawed and cut. After handing out bait to groups of people around the boat, I explained how to work the reels so they didn't backlash the spools and told people about the fish they could expect to catch.

Once we arrived at the fishing grounds, I'd help bait the women's hooks (and sometimes the men's), gaff the fish caught, and bring the fish aboard. We'd assign marks to each person and cut Roman numerals on top of the fish heads, which I thought was cool, so that person could claim their fish at the end of the day.

I'd also fillet the catch for tips, which is where I made most of my money. I became very good at it and as a young boy began to build up a pretty good bank account, making $10–20 in tips each day. Then I'd fillet the leftover fish no one wanted, put them in a big cooler, and peddle them to tourists. I even knocked on doors in the trailer park where we had our summer home, selling fish for a dollar a fillet. I sold everything as haddock, regardless of what species it really was, and worked seven days a week from June to the end of August. I loved every minute of it and never once considered it a job. I just thought I was the luckiest kid in the world. Even though my parents had virtually no interest in fishing or any sort of ocean-going life, they never tried to talk me out of this. They knew I was extremely happy and were 100 percent supportive.

What I remember the most of those early days working for Al Voorhis is getting busted stealing a ham sandwich. Actually, it was three sandwiches.

My mother would pack lunch each day for both Al and me. On those rare days when my mom would have an off day, we wouldn't have enough food to sustain us so I would go out and pillage and plunder for sandwiches and other cooler goodies. I always fantasized I was a pirate back then. Sometimes I still do.

I can close my eyes and remember this like it just happened. It became one of the few times I've ever panicked. I was really hungry and Al was even more so.

"Go round up some sandwiches, Corky," he said. "What happened, did your mom sleep in this morning? I think you might have to start waking her up earlier."

Off I went in search of lunch. I looked in a couple of coolers brought by guests that were tucked away out of anyone's sight. There was nothing really interesting until I found a large bag full of great big ham sandwiches. I grabbed two and started to close the bag when I became greedy and reached back in for a third, breaking Al's rule of grab and split.

I unwrapped that third sandwich and sat right down to eat it when the owner of the bag came into the old galley and caught me. He got really mad and I freaked out. I wanted to bolt and run, but you can't run far on a boat.

I'm dead, I thought to myself.

I immediately confessed, but told the man I stole his food because the Captain made me. I said if I didn't bring him a sandwich he'd, he'd—well, I didn't know what, but it would be real bad. This sounded perfect to my eight-year-old ears, but it must have sounded ridiculous to the man because he took me right to Al.

I vividly remember Al being scared and white as a sheet. He denied it all and I couldn't believe what he was telling this man. He said he didn't even know who I was and that I must be a stowaway or something.

"Where's your father young man? You should be ashamed," he said to me. "Sorry sir, but I gotta move the boat. Not enough fish," he said to the man. "Everyone up," he yelled at the top of his lungs, dismissing me to this really mad man.

At the end of this whole nightmare I remember asking the man if I could have the rest of that sandwich. He threw it overboard. In turn, I filleted his fish for free.

My summer earnings went into buying my own school clothes, which I took great pride in, and it also kept me in motorcycles. But by the end of the school year I'd have spent all the previous summer's savings. At an early age the bad habit of spending money as fast as I made it had started—something fishermen are famous for.

As I reflect back on these first four years, I realize I learned a lot from the old man, although not necessarily good things. One lesson that has had a profound effect on me my whole adult life has been dishonesty. He'd tell a tourist the damnest things. In the afternoon and early evenings Al and I would lean up against his shiny black Caddie that had a homemade sign cut out to look like a cod. *Deep Sea Fishing*

Onboard the Marion it would beckon. We'd talk to tourists, make reservations for the following day, and lie.

"How was the fishing today?" Joe tourist would ask.

"It really sucked," I'd start to say, as Al's vice-like grip squeezed into my thin shoulders like a lobster clamping down on an unexpecting finger.

"Unbelievable. We loaded the boat," Al told the man, when we had actually caught around eight fish for thirty people. "You and the missus want to come tomorrow? We got room."

"Tell them what they want to hear, what's the matter with you?" he'd reprimand me afterwards, before asking, "Got anything to eat?"

These early years shaped me and started the turn down a slippery gangway that I've struggled with my whole life. I don't believe in a lot of things, but I do believe that we choose our own path in life, with events and certain people playing a role in guiding us along the way. I was raised better, yet I chose to walk down this path. I knew what I was doing even at nine years old as I sold a cusk fillet as haddock to a sixty-year-old woman. I was headed down a dishonest road and, frankly, didn't care. I accepted it as the way of life as a fisherman. It would take me another 30 years to finally figure out that dishonesty has a way of eventually catching up with you.

At the age of twelve and the beginning of my fifth summer in Maine, I asked Al Voorhis to pay me. When he gave me an emphatic "nope," I jumped ship and went to work for the competition, Jack Miller, on his charter boat the *Seahawk*. Jack paid me $20 a week, and in truth I made way more in tips with Al. It was a respect issue. I felt I was worth a weekly paycheck and receiving one made a difference.

Each day while I cleaned up and put away the *Seahawk*, my buddies working on the tuna boats would land at the bait dock and hoist giant bluefin tuna off their decks. Their stories of days spent chasing giant bluefins around Jefferies Ledge drew me in like a starving labrador to a rare sirloin steak. What could be cooler than throwing poles at an 800-pound fish? Even though I stayed with Jack three years, the lure of fishing for bluefin tuna consumed my thoughts. I yearned to become a part of tuna fever.

TUNA FEVER

The bluefin tuna harpooners of Perkins Cove were and probably still are the best in the world. During the summer of 1977, I was fascinated by these great fish that Sonny McIntyre, the Wiener Brothers, and other harpooners were bringing into town. All my friends at the cove lived and breathed tuna, and I longed to join them.

It wasn't until the following summer, at sixteen years old, that I finally had my chance. I arrived back for my family's summer in Maine hungry for a tuna position. The cove guys are a very tight group and jobs were very hard to come by for someone who didn't have any experience—and that was me. Harpooning requires only two people, one to drive the boat and one to throw the pole, making opportunities slim. Determined, I asked, begged, and pleaded with every boat that had a pulpit stand to iron (harpoon) the tuna from to take me along on a trip. The best I was offered was, "Sure, come along any time." This wasn't a job offer; it just allowed me to be a spectator.

With tuna season fast approaching, I heard Old Man Young was going to put a pulpit on his dragger (trawler), so I went to see him. The old man ate crew for breakfast. He was mean, ornery, and went through a lot of guys. I was desperate.

Ken Young, Sr., was in his late-sixties and his boat, the *Ugly Anne* (named after his ex-wife), was a 42-foot wooden dragger. It wasn't an ideal stick boat, but I didn't know any better. At the time he was just as desperate for crew as I was for a job. He knew of me, but didn't have a clue about what I actually knew and didn't want to pay a full share. Even though he told me dragging was his living and tuna fishing would be something to play around with on nice days, I signed on.

Finally, I had my chance. Arriving home that night I was very excited, but also for the first time nervous. Going into commercial fishing was totally different from making money off tourists. If we didn't catch fish, we didn't get paid.

The next day I rode my bicycle to Ken's house at 4 a.m. and found him waiting with the pickup running. I jumped in and immediately started to ask a million questions. He finally told me to shut up and that I'd find out soon enough. I don't really think I could be quiet though, and after a couple of minutes another "must know" question had to be asked.

We arrived at York Harbor, a small port with only a few other dragger men walking about that morning. Soon we were out through the river and headed for the fishing grounds outside Noble lighthouse. We were going to tow for blackback and yellowtail flounders inshore, a half mile or so from the beach.

I received a quick lesson on how to get the net off the reel and hooked up to the trawl doors and how to operate the main winches. I thought I didn't do too badly, but in reality I managed to set about 15 feet too much on one side. After the old man evened out the marks, with none too little cursing, we were towing.

This wasn't tuna fishing and I wasn't really closer to my dream, but it was a new experience and I was excited, happy, and eager to learn all I could. After a couple of hours we were ready to haul back the net. With another winch lesson I managed to get the doors to the towing blocks hanging from the gallest frames in the stern section without any serious damage. With a little help and some more ass chewing, we got the slack wire on the trawl doors hooked up to the reel and were able to wind the ground gear and net up. About 1,000 pounds of mixed flatfish were dumped on deck, along with a few cod and haddock.

After we set out the net for another tow, the flatfish needed to be separated by species and size, and the round fish needed to be gilled and gutted. I looked at the pile of fish and then looked at the old man with what must have been a real pained expression, since I didn't have a clue about which sole was which or how to size them. I did know the cod and haddock though, and proudly told him so. This sent the old guy in orbit. I had never heard some of the words I was called that day, but I sure learned the difference between a blackback and a yellowtail flounder fast.

Once the fish were sorted we placed them in tote containers. We threw some ice from the hole on top of them and stored the totes on the deck. I survived that day and quickly learned the bottomfish fishery. After a few trips under my belt, I became good at it. That is until we tore up. Oh man. I learned how to hold the twine to repair the net for the old man because every time I got off I'd get the needle slapped over my knuckles with a crack.

"Stay awake and keep over the lay of the twine," he'd growl.

I quickly grew afraid of the old man and avoided him as much as possible, which is kind of hard on a 40-foot boat. I spent a lot of time on deck. Finally, around the end of June he announced that we were going to put the stand on, meaning the pulpit. Oh my God. I couldn't believe it. We were rigging up for tuna.

Late in the day when the stand was finally in place, the old man went home. The boat was at the lower dock under the bridge at Perkins Cove and I ventured out onto the pulpit and practiced throwing a harpoon until dark. I was in heaven, even though the job of actually throwing the pole at a fish was the old man's. I was finally living a dream.

The next two summers were spent with Ken. We did spend some days looking for tuna, but never caught a single fish. In reality, we never even threw the pole once in two years and spent very little time trying.

We were not good at it, had no tower or mast, and drove the boat from the roof of the house. Because of this, we probably drove by a hundred bunches those years without ever seeing them.

What those two summers did give me, however, was experience at the dragging business, along with insight to the tuna game.

TUNA

Changes in the 70s

The 1970s were tumultuous times for tuna fishermen on the East Coast. They hit hard times when Japanese longliners were allowed to fish U.S. waters and catch all the fish that the Japanese market demanded. This left the American tuna fishermen to peddle their fish to local markets in Boston and New York for very little money. Sometimes they even resorted to selling these great fish for dog and cat food. Management of the fishery became critical to their financial survival. Sonny McIntyre, a tuna highliner and the best harpooner to ever throw a pole, once told me he caught four fish and called in an ice truck to deliver his fish to Boston. The fish sold for less than the trucking bill. He delivered over 2,000 pounds of bluefin and ended up with owing the truck driver.

With the advent of the Magnuson-Stevens Fishery Conservation and Management Act in April of 1976, the U.S. government finally took steps to protect our own fishermen, limiting the Japanese to a small quota of fish. All of a sudden, foreigners had to buy fish from us, the American fishermen. Tuna was now worth something and fish began to sell for upwards of a dollar a pound. By 1996, I heard of a single fish caught in Nova Scotia that was put into a holding pen to fatten up selling for over $40,000, and $20 a pound was not uncommon for a fish in perfect condition with a high fat content.

Still, the latter 1970s had its share of stumbling blocks, including provisions required by the International Commission for the Conservation of Atlantic Tuna (ICCAT). It placed a moratorium on bluefin, making it illegal to catch more than one fish a day. Before this, harpooners would spend all summer waiting for the day when they had perfect conditions and could iron eight, nine, ten or more fish. Limiting fishermen to one fish a day did not go over well. A compromise was finally reached where harpooners agreed to participate in a tagging program. We used our harpoon poles, but switched out the darts and replaced them with sharpened plastic tags that would be imbedded in tuna after we had caught our fish for the day. Every time we tagged a fish, we'd record the tag number, date, time, and location. The purpose was to help scientists learn about their migratory patterns, since very little was known about bluefin tuna at that time.

For every five fish tagged, we would get a chit good for the harvest of one tuna. These chits could be used after August 20, when the regulations went from one a day to seven a week. If a boat tagged thirty fish during the summer, it was allowed six additional fish to be caught anytime after August 20, when they also were allowed to harvest their allotted seven for the week.

This program lasted two years. I started my tuna career in 1978, in the second year of the program. The major problem was it was set up on the honor system. Each boat was assigned a certain number of tags. Once a tuna was tagged, the data would be given to the National Marine Fisheries Service and we would collect our chits.

In those two summers a lot of bluefin were tagged and some very interesting data was obtained. Timmy Tower tagged a fish in June 1977 off Boon Island, Maine, and the following fall it was caught off of Sicily, Italy. Fish were swimming across the Atlantic Ocean into the Mediterranean.

The bluefin, however, weren't the only fish those two summers that had ended up with brightly colored tags stuck to them. We tagged everything that swam, including ocean sunfish, blue dogs (blue sharks), basking sharks, and pilot whales. If it swam on the surface, it was fair game. And of course we claimed them all as tagged bluefin. I remember seeing one ocean sunfish that was decorated with about a dozen such tags. The fish looked like a Christmas tree. The Feds eventually got wise to this game. A plane was hired and in the summer of 1978 a few busts were made, but eventually the program was just discarded.

This is where I first learned about the government's involvement in a fishery by regulating it in a bad way. In this particular case, it meant we were allowed one fish a day. As fishermen, we either live by the law and stay within the guidelines, or we tag a blue dog and report it as a bluefin. Did all harpooners do this back then? Nope. But I do know with bad fisheries management comes bad fishing and dishonest fishing practices.

More changes in the fishery came around in 1979, and three categories consisting of harpoon, general, and seine were set up with separate quotas. The harpoon category was allotted around 80 metric tons of catch for a quota, which allowed each boat to catch as many fish as it could each day by harpoon. The general category had a catch quota of around 600 metric tons, but was only allowed one fish to be caught a day, whether by harpoon, hand line, or rod and reel. The seine category included six boats that were grandfathered in for method seining with a quota of 600 metric tons, and no other boats could enter this fishery.

This was the start of the modern day tuna fleet. The days when tuna fishing was a sport for the rich or a change of pace for lobstermen and draggers were changing. The opportunity to make real money chasing these magnificent fish had arrived.

TO CATCH A TUNA

By 1980, I couldn't take another summer of Old Man Young's abuse and got a job on another dragger. This time the skipper was very serious about harpooning tuna. The late Brian Burke's 35-foot Bruno was rigged for both dragging and harpooning. We went dragging in two spots—off the beach and Boon Island ledge—which were the only two spots I think Brian knew. When the end of June rolled around, off came the drag gear and on came the pulpit.

In Brian's case, the pulpit was a 16-foot wooden plank reinforced with guide wires and a belly rail. We had a mast with rope steering and a set of Morse controls in the mast. Although this was a very primitive set-up, Brian was hard core. Like the rest of the cove tuna men, we would follow fish from Rhode Island to the most northern tip of Maine, living like nomads up and down the coast. We were ready to catch some bluefin.

The first couple of days we didn't see any fish, but Eric Braizer got one and Timmy Tower another. These first two fish of the year were both singles, traveling alone rather than in schools. On our third day, the first of July, we headed offshore on a flat calm day. As we passed Boon Island ledge I spotted a huge whitewater wake called a coma plowing along, indicating a tuna. I couldn't believe it and just pointed.

Brian looked over and screamed in my ear, "Fish!" He slowed the boat down and was out on the stand before I even realized he was gone.

I moved over to the mast where the controls were, sped the boat up a little, and grabbed the two lines that steered the boat. It felt like I'd been doing this my whole life as we rode up behind that fish. Brian waited until the fish was practically under his feet. I couldn't frigging believe he was waiting so long. All I could think about was wanting him to throw the pole.

Finally, with Brian's body blocking my view of the fish, he threw. A huge splash was followed by an enormous amount of whitewater and spray. The oak harpoon pole exploded in a half dozen pieces or more and floated by us, piece by piece, as the line went out. He had hit the fish.

I grabbed the microphone to the VHF radio and announced to the world, "We got one!" at the top of my lungs. Brian just looked at me, shaking his head, probably wondering how in the hell he ever ended up with this kid on his boat.

Soon the fish came to the end of the warp and we put a flag out to mark the fish. The fish towed the flag for about ten minutes before it stopped and was dead. We rigged a second pole just in case the dart pulled out when the fish came next to the boat, and hauled in 100 fathoms of warp.

I was on the just in case pole.

"Okay, here he comes," Brian said, as soon as we saw the fish.

All I hear is okay. With blood pumping through my veins, I drove the harpoon as hard as I could into the fish, double darting the dead beast.

"What are you doing?" Brian asked incredulously.

I just looked at him with what I can only imagine was a crazed look and said, "you said okay."

Brian stared at me for a long moment before finally shaking his head and looking off. He was probably wondering how he was going to survive the summer with this kid.

The fish weighed over 700 pounds dressed, which was a big fish for so early in the season. I received a check for $265, which was 25 percent of the value of the fish when it sold for at $1.50 a pound. Oh man, was I hooked.

That summer the tuna were in a very small area called the prong, which was a ledge near Jeffreys Bank. They were big fish, but became very spooky from being chased and no one caught too many. The Weiners got twenty or so, Sonny McIntyre caught about fifteen, and Riley, Dana, Brazier, and the rest of the highliners all also caught about the same. We caught seven for the season. We pulled a few darts and lost the fish, but missed even more. Quite a few were barn doors and should have been easy ones to hit. I didn't make much money for college that fall, but it was the best summer I could ever have imagined in my young life so far. Even more important, the other fishermen accepted me as one of them. I was finally part of the gang.

That year in college went by quickly, even though I didn't do too well because I spent most of my time dreaming of fishing for tuna. Memories like the truckloads of Miller cans we consumed (and that Brian was famous for) lingered in my mind. He would never leave the dock without at least a case of beer. Brian would insist on three things when it came to beer: it had to be Miller, it had to be in a can, and it needed to be lots. I also thought about different ports we visited. Summer couldn't come quick enough.

I finished finals the first part of May in 1981 and was back in Ogunquit the next day. I had a job lined up with Eric Brazier lobstering and tuna fishing and moved into The Cove apartments with my best friend from growing up, Bobby McIntyre. Our apartment was just a few short steps to the docks and it promised to be a great summer.

Eric was a second-generation tuna fisherman and was one of the best. His usual deckhand was going to the Maine Maritime Academy, so I snapped up the job even though I felt bad about leaving Brian. We started the summer season fishing for lobster and I soon learned hauling lobster traps was not for me. It was very demanding work and Eric paid only $50 a day. We hauled around 300 traps a day, from 5 a.m. to 4–6 p.m. at night.

Eric was a very demanding boss and there was little time off. If we weren't hauling pots he'd have me building them at his house or dipping wooden larves (sections of pots) and whole pots in a mixture of chemicals so that sea worms wouldn't eat the oak. Today the Environmental Protection Agency would flat out shoot you if you tried mixing up a batch of the trap dip. Eric would also have me painting buoys, mowing his lawn, and even cleaning his garage. I did it all and never complained. Well, almost never.

I got teased a lot by the other guys who would ask, "Cork, are you babysitting, mowing lawns, or actually fishing today?" But tuna season was coming.

We rigged Eric's boat, a 38-foot Young Brothers with a large Volvo diesel that in those days was considered fast. Eric had a 16-foot fiberglass one-of-a-kind stand he built and the tower was state of the art with a trick hydro steering system. Our harpoon gear consisted of a dozen balanced harpoon poles with eight flag ends and warps. Everything was the best money could buy.

The first day out we headed for the prong where all the action took place the summer before. It was early June and a flat calm day. On the VHF radio reports were coming in from other boats. We heard Brian had missed a couple of singles and Brooksie saw a small bunch, so there were a few fish around. We saw Brian about a half mile away in an area we had passed through out on the stand. Another chance, another miss.

Then Eric spotted a single running very light and making a small wake. We got right up on it and Eric placed a perfect hit behind the dorsal fin on top of the fish. We had our first flag of the year out. Spot one fish, one chance, one hit, and we boated the fish within an hour. We were off to a great start. The fish was small, weighing about 450 pounds dressed, but it was the first fish caught that year on the Eastern seaboard and we were proud. Usually the Cape Cod boys have a few in before the Mainers.

We had five fish by the first week in July. The first day of July we went to Middle Banks and boated a fish just before a huge fog bank settled over the area. The flag went into the water just as a line of thick chalky white fog engulfed us. I remember driving from the mast straining to keep my eye on the flag end, which was being towed around 8 knots by the fish.

Eric was still in the stand yelling at me not to lose the flag. I never took my eyes off it for a second and thank Christ it quickly came to a sudden halt. The fish, luckily for us, died a fast death and we pulled up to the drifting buoy as Eric came out of the stand pulling the flag end onboard the bow. As I came out of the mast to help, I remember looking around thinking holy shit, we are frigging lost. The fog was so thick you couldn't see a boat length in any direction. It was surreal and spooky and I felt like we were in a movie set or something. This was a time before global positioning systems (GPS), where even every skiff on the planet has a handheld location device. Back then we had nothing but Loran C, a long-range electronic positioning system based on the shoreline, a paper chart, and a magnetic compass.

We found our way into Gloucester that night by following a charter boat into the breakwater and we weren't the only guys following our guide. The rod and reel guys, along with all the stick boats, the Maine Boys, and most of the guys from the Cape were lined up bow to stern. When we made it to shore we had a huge party at the Tri-Coastal Seafood docking area, where beer and stories flowed late into the night.

The next morning dawned bright and sunny as about thirty hungover harpooners made their way out past the breakwater in the early morning light. We heard a huge handline fleet had been chumming fish up and were harvesting tons of big fish, so we went looking for bunches outside of them. A very light west wind tempered the hot sun and made it a picture perfect day for a stick boat.

Eric had an old friend, Bobby, join us that week. He was better known as BoBo. We had just arrived at the area where we had ironed yesterday's fish when I spotted six fish coming up to the surface to run. I maneuvered behind the bunch and Eric picked the fish he wanted. By 9 a.m. we had a flag out. Eric was rigging up another pole when the bunch popped right back up. Bang, we had number two out. Both flags were heading offshore in the same direction, so we followed, looking for more. By this time all the stick boats had arrived in the area and no one else was seeing any fish. The bunch didn't show again, but that didn't stop about fifty stick boats from running every which way, all over the top of us. There were so many boats in such a small area that the fish in the area had no chance to even make it to the surface.

We decided to go check our flags. The first fish, a 500-pounder, was dead and we soon had him boated. I bled the fish and tarped him as BoBo and Eric cleaned off the deck and put away the warp and flag. I was back in the mast running towards the second flag when a single appeared about two boat lengths in front of us. I screamed for Eric and he ran out onto the stand in bare feet and no sunglasses. He had been changing from boots to sneakers when I yelled. He grabbed the pole as he positioned himself on the stand and made an unbelievable throw at a fish that was on its way to being gone. We had number three out, and it wasn't even noon yet. I was going nuts.

We proceeded to check number two, a 300-pounder. It was dead and soon tarped off next to the first. We went to check number three, which had been hit high in the side near its head. It was hurt and was swimming near the surface in circles. From the mast it appeared to be a big fish. We tried to get up to it twice to iron it again, but couldn't get close enough before it went down. Brooks Weiner rode up on the fish later not realizing it was ours and almost stuck it before he saw the line trailing from it. He would have saved us one hell of a fight later in the day if he would have.

We thought it best to leave it and hope it would die while we went looking for another. From what we were hearing on the radio, no other fish were being caught or even seen, yet we had two in the boat and one out. Eric decided to head to the south side of the handline fleet. He didn't think the third fish would travel far and we had a good position fixed on it with our Loran. The area we were in had way too many boats. As we made our way around the chummers, another stick boat took off steaming towards a bunch of fish, so we followed them and watched from one-half mile as the bunch settled near the boat. We figured it might be a good area to look.

The other boat never even saw the fish when Eric spotted the bunch it was chasing pop up right behind them. We waited five minutes for the fish to settle down, and then took off after them. It was a nice bunch of fifteen to eighteen fish running strong. We made an approach and talked Eric onto a fish lagging behind, riding right up on it. The fish was a barn door and number four was out. It died within ten minutes and we boated another 500-pounder.

We arrived back to our number three flag at around 4 p.m., with the fish still alive and swimming in circles. We'd have to fight this one. The shotgun was loaded and another harpoon rigged. We took hold of the warp and started to ease the fish towards the boat, but every time the fish saw the boat it would dive and take off with all the line we fought to gain. The battle went on until 6 p.m., with the three of us becoming very tired while the fish didn't seem tired at all. Eric managed to turn the fish towards the stern of our boat. He had the fish just up to the throwing line about sixty feet out when the fish swam towards us. I was holding the second harpoon and threw it at the speeding fish as it streaked by the stern. It hit the fish about six inches up from the base of its tail, even though I know I threw twenty feet in front of it.

We now had the second dart in him and debated whether to set the flags back out. We decided to hold onto him and fight it out. The second line seemed to take the fight out of the fish and we had him alongside in thirty minutes. It was a monster, dwarfing the other three, and ended up dressing out at 880 pounds.

We made Gloucester an hour after dark. We had four chances that day, four hits, and four fish. We were perfect that day and the only boat to land any fish in the harpoon category. It was unheard of. When the rest of the fleet strikes out a boat may get one or maybe two fish, but four never happens. We were off to an unbelievable start. It was the first week of July and we had nine fish to our credit—already two more than all of last summer.

The next day Eric's brother and his son came out with us and we boated two more. The following day Eric and I headed back to Ogunquit to haul his lobster gear, which had been soaking for over four weeks. I was devastated and couldn't believe we were leaving. We had just caught seven fish in three days and we were going lobstering?

I can now understand why we had to go tend those pots. If you have $30,000 worth of gear in the water you just don't forget about it. Eric was a family man with a newborn son. Being away for extended times was tough. At the time, however, I was very bitter—especially since I had just made over $2,000 in three days. I was extremely pumped up by the luck we were having. We were the hot boat in the fleet. My relationship with Eric became seriously strained as I found myself back hauling pots for $50 a day while I heard stories of big days on other boats.

That summer during the Bailey Island tuna tournament the Cobra had an eleven-fish day. It was a hot summer. Sonny McIntyre caught over sixty fish that year. On Eric's boat we did fish for more tuna that summer, but only on certain perfect days. Eric was only a part-time tuna fisherman. He was very wealthy and being away from his family and lobster pots in order to be a nomad for two months chasing tuna was too much of a sacrifice to him. We ended up with seventeen fish for the year and I went back to college bitter, knowing it could have been one great year.

For the summer of 1982, I hooked up with George Wyman, an old ex-Marine from Bailey Island. George was building a new 32-foot Holland with a local boat finisher. It was going to be extremely fast and built just for tuna fishing. George assured me we would live and breathe tuna and that his boat would never see a lobster.

George was the most stubborn man I'd ever met and his temper was scary. Once he had an idea, he would stick with it no matter what. We chased fish all summer but spent most it either in Perkins Cove or his homeport of Bailey Island, even though most of the fish were ironed off of Massachusetts that year.

Bailey Island is a small quiet coastal town north of Portland, Maine. It is the home of lobstermen and a few draggers and is locally famous for Mackerel Cove Marina. The marina has changed owners a few times, but when I was there it was owned by a man named Bill and his wife and two daughters. During the summer of 1982 I spent a lot of time there and his family treated me like one of their own.

The following year when we showed up, Bill had some great shirts made up for the bar and restaurant staff. It was a red shirt with a picture of a tuna and Mackerel Cove printed over the breast pocket. When I asked Bill for a shirt he refused and told me you had to either work there or sleep with someone who worked there to get one of the shirts. When I arrived for breakfast the next morning wearing one of those red shirts, Bill went nuts and kept looking over at his oldest daughter and his niece. I refused to tell him how I got that shirt, but he knew damn well that I wasn't on his pay sheet.

The cove held an annual Bailey Island Tuna Tournament the last week of July. Boats came from all around New England, transforming this quiet little town into drunken, crazed madness for one week each year. Boats rafted six to eight boats deep with all-night parties and general craziness. In some years back in the 1970s and early 1980s lots of tuna were landed. Prizes in the form of trophies and money were given out for fish caught by a rod and reel, harpoon, handline, largest, most, smallest, and largest by harpoon. It was an event we all looked forward to each year.

This year we won the Bailey Island tuna tournament and caught one of only two fish. Ours was the biggest and won in three categories: the largest, most, and largest by harpoon. Yet by summer's end we finished with only nine fish and only had one multiple fish day, when we caught three at the end of August. It was a tough summer. I was never truly happy with George and was relieved to head back to school.

I didn't know it, but this would be my last full year in college. I spent more time at Sugarloaf ski area that winter than in classes, changed my major I don't know how many times, and was doing very poorly. When school let out the first part of May, I returned to fishing.

I went to work for Jerry Fraser dragging on his 42-foot Bruno. I decided that dragging was going to be my livelihood and focused all my attention on it. I learned how to tow and mend and all I could about the industry from Jerry. I was planning on fishing all summer with Jerry and to forego tuna fishing this year. My plan was to buckle down, save some money, and become responsible. Yeah right.

By the end of June I broke the news to Jerry that I'd be leaving his boat, but told him I'd be back at the end of summer when the tuna season was over if he'd have me, and I wasn't planning on returning to college. Jerry wasn't surprised. He knew I had the fever and told me I could work through the winter if he had a spot open.

I passed up a job with Dana Kangas out of Gloucester, one of the best tuna fishermen anywhere, to be able to stay in southern Maine. I ended up going with Glen Goodwin from Kennebunkport. Glen's boat was an old twin screw classic built for one purpose—harpooning. It was a great old boat with a lot of history.

The *Bomba C* was originally the *Susan* built by Jack Cadario in the late 1960s. He sold the boat to the Goodwins when he had the *Cobra* built in the early 1970s. The boat was built of wood that Glen had fiberglassed over. It had a huge pulpit over twenty feet long with a tall step-style tower. While the boat wasn't real fast, it was a great stick boat.

We worked on the boat the last couple of weeks in June and were ready the first of July. The cove guys had already caught a few fish, but we didn't miss much. We went for a shakedown out towards Boon Island and had a chance at a deep running bunch, but missed. We went the entire month of July without a fish. We pulled four darts that month and missed quite a few shots—some easy, and some that were desperate throws. Peanut butter sandwiches were our main diet. It wasn't that we didn't have chances. We just blew them.

At the end of July, we were so broke that we had to borrow money for fuel from Glen's dad. We departed Bailey Island at the close of the tournament and headed back to Kennebunkport. We were going across Jeffrey's Ledge when we saw a bunch up running. As we got behind the school I noticed that the fish didn't look very big, but there were a lot of them. I talked Glen onto the largest fish I could see, and we finally broke the ice.

We had a flag out and the fish didn't go very far before the flag stopped. Glen and I looked at each other, afraid that we had just pulled another dart. We started to pull in the slack warp and a little tension became apparent, but it was nothing like you would feel pulling in 500 or so pounds of dead bluefin. Puzzled, we kept it coming. Soon the throwing line appeared and then this little butterball fish popped to the surface. It was the smallest bluefin I'd ever seen, and it was the big fish in the bunch. The fish dressed out at a massive 70 pounds. We didn't even use the tuna door. We just pulled the little guy over the rail by hand, something I'd never heard of happening before.

We toasted the fish with two bottles of beer we were saving for the first fish. Sure enough, that little guy changed our luck. We caught thirteen more fish in the next three weeks and in September managed to get three more down on the Cape that sold for a lot. I think we made around $4 pound and the summer ended up being a good one.

By the end of September I was back in Ogunquit knocking on Jerry's door. Jerry was buying a bigger boat, a 63-foot eastern rig. It was a type that I had never stepped foot on before, but I was game. I later found out that Jerry had never fished on one either and we learned it together. The *Princess* was built in the late 1940s and I soon learned why these boats were called dinosaur rigs.

An eastern-rigged dragger is a traditional trawler. Unlike today's modern high horsepower stern trawlers, the eastern rig is a side trawler with gallest frames on the same side of the vessel. The *Princess* was definitely traditional and had a GMC 871 main engine with a manual power take off which operated an old chain drive Hathaway winch. It was a beautiful old vessel with classic lines, but also had the horsepower of a sewing machine.

I fished with Jerry for the next ten months. We didn't get rich, but made a decent living by delivering four- to seven-day trips into Portsmouth and Gloucester. Jerry taught me a lot that winter and gave me a lot of responsibility. He would let me dock the boat, make daily tows, and taught me navigation. I learned more from Jerry than any other person I had ever fished with. He was a great influence and became a good friend. Nonetheless, for a second time I told Jerry my plans to go chase tuna and gave him my notice.

I went to work that summer for Jack Cadario on his boat out of Nashua, New Hampshire. He owned the *Cobra*, a 45-foot wooden boat made out of African mahogany with teak decks and rails. It had a big 24-foot pulpit with a 40-foot mast that towered over everything else in the fleet. Since I was a child I had held that boat in awe.

I started work in early June, helping to get the *Cobra* ready for summer. I soon learned how much work it took to keep a classic wooden boat looking as good as the *Cobra*. Old paint was scraped, paint remover applied, and then coats of primer were used before applying the final coats of paint.

Jack took a great amount of pride in his boat, and for good reason. It was a beautiful boat. If a job wasn't done to his satisfaction, it was done over. I did many jobs twice. We sanded, painted, oiled teak, cleaned, and went over equipment for a month. When we were done the boat looked beautiful. On our shakedown cruise we ironed a nice fish to christen the boat and start off the summer.

Jack planned to spend the summer on the backside of Cape Cod off of Rhode Island and New York. He figured we could take a few swordfish along with tuna. It was my first time this far south. We visited Nantucket, Martha's Vineyard, Provincetown (on the tip of Cape Cod), Block Island, Fairhaven, and New Bedford. We also fished the south tip of Georges Bank. The *Cobra* was big enough to have a fish hole and we took about five tons of ice with us, which let us stay out three or four days at a time. On the south side of Cape Cod the Gulf Stream comes inshore and the water is considerably warmer. We saw sharks I'd never seen before, including hammerheads, makos, poor beagles, and even a great white.

Jack and I were together in the tower idling along when we both glanced down and saw this huge shark about ten feet off the side of the boat, swimming alongside us. It was so big I thought it might be a basking shark; a harmless plankton-eating giant. The shark rolled partway onto its side and we could see a white belly and a good profile of its head and its solid black eye. It was no basking shark. It was a great white.

Jack and I looked at each other and I imagine he could see the whites of my eyes through my sunglasses. "Jesus Christ," we said together, as we both reached for the throttles. When we glanced back, the shark was gone.

Other species we saw were sea turtles and marlin, which Jack called skillies. I think they were white or striped marlin. They were about five feet long, weighed around 100 pounds, and looked a lot like swordfish when they were finning. They sure faked us out.

We did manage to iron quite a few marlins, although they were a small target with only about a foot across the back and very hard to hit. These fish were great on the barbeque and we sold them for about $1–1.50 a pound locally, which angered the sport fishermen to no end, who prized these fish for their rod and reel clients.

We also saw yellowfin, albacore, skipjack, and, of course, bluefin tuna. The only swordfish we saw that summer was the one we boated. It weighed just under 200 pounds dressed. Up to this time, we had fourteen bluefin below the Cape and they were all small 200–300 pound fish. We did see a few giants, but not many.

One day in early August on the southern tip of Georges Bank, we spotted the largest school of bluefin I've ever heard of. They were all 150–300 pound fish and there were thousands. The bunch was running and covered an area over a mile. We put out seven flags before we drove the bunch down and had to go back to our gear.

The old man never left the stand. When we'd iron a fish, I'd set the flag overboard and run another harpoon out to him. We boated five of the seven. It was incredible putting out those seven flags. It lasted a total of maybe thirty to forty-five minutes and was total madness. When it was over we looked back behind the boat and it looked like a golf course with our buoys everywhere.

We received word that the harpoon category was going to close in mid-August and we had about a week to go. We decided to head to Provincetown and finish off the season in the bay. We took two more fish before the season closed, both large 700-pounders. We ended the season with twenty-three bluefin, one swordfish, and a handful of yellowfin tuna and marlin. It was the middle of August and we were done.

Everyone was trying to line up boats that were registered in the general category, but Jack had another business to run and was done for the year. I scrambled to find a boat and hooked up with Lex and Ron from Monhegan Island, Maine. I was pretty much just going along for the ride until I could find another paying job. We caught five fish with an old stick boat that Lex somehow located.

In early September in Perkins Cove, I met up with George Wyman. He had a new boat and it was registered in the general category. The last few summers had mellowed George and we got along like father and son. We finished off the summer together until the general category was closed down in late September. We ended up with four nice fish which all sold for top dollar, which in those days meant around $4 a pound.

Those were the last four tuna I'd ever see taken. At the time I thought I'd die with a harpoon in my hand and I'd chase tuna until my last breath. Harpooning is to me the purest, most rewarding fishery in the world. Something so primitive as throwing a pole at a fish is a beautiful way to fish. It is clean, simple, and thrilling as you go one-on-one, man against fish.

Even in this most basic fishery I broke the law and felt zero guilt and absolutely no respect for the fisheries management laws. This early disrespect, rightly so or not, became the building blocks for what I ended up paying dearly for seventeen years later.

In the fall, I skipped college again and went fishing with Cory Goodwin, Glen's younger brother, dragging and shrimping on his 55-foot Bruno. Cory promised me a chance to run his boat when he'd take trips off, and we fished out of Kennebunkport that fall and winter. In November we rigged up for shrimp and made day trips out to Boon Island. I got to run the boat about a dozen trips that winter and did very good for my first crack at it. The money wasn't great, but we made a decent week's pay.

Throughout the winter I kept hearing from my little sister about how friends of hers at school were making money—big money—fishing summers in Alaska. Finally, my father got involved and did some research about the different fisheries up there. He knew I was not getting ahead in Maine and started to put pressure on me to try Alaska. I was very reluctant. I was finally getting a chance to run a boat and there was tuna fishing to look forward to.

In March of 1985, after another long telephone conversation with my dad in which he offered the kind of courage, faith, and confidence that only a father can, I decided to give it a try. I thought if I didn't like Alaska I could still make it home to Maine in time for tuna season.

Always in the background was J.B., who also offered her own special encouragement. She was an inspiration for adventure, having herself left for a distant college in Alaska at the young age of eighteen. She was known as the student going the farthest away to college from Wahconah High School in Pittsfield, Massachusetts, where we lived during the school year and our dad was now the principal. She was brave. I figured what the hell, if she could do it, so could I.

*   *   *

I haven't caught a bluefin since 1985, but I have kept up on the fishery and its problems, concerns, and the challenges that face today's bluefin fishermen. If you talk to the scientists from Woods Hole, they'll tell you the fish population has crashed and the giants are a thing of the past, having all been caught in the old days by guys like me. If you talk to a Cape Cod stick boat, they aren't ironing many fish in the bay these days. Instead, they're running offshore around the point of Provincetown as far as the southern tip of Georges Bank in search of bunches of fish. Huge rafts of bluefin can still be found. They just move on and don't stick around an area like they did in the 1970s. A rod and reel guy from Gloucester told me he racked up over a hundred fish in 2007. Granted they may not all be giants, but there are still huge numbers of bluefin being caught.

Jerry Fraser, who eventually left fishing and became the editor in chief of the *National Fisherman* magazine, told me that the Maine and Novi Scotia guys had a huge three-day span one August, where the harpoon and rod and reel boats just numbed them and the bluefin caught were all big fish. There are some good success stories that oppose the opinion of some scientists. Fishermen know the fish are still out there, but their migration patterns, holding areas, and behavior have changed significantly over the last twenty years.

It takes a lot of bait to fatten up an Atlantic bluefin that swims up the Gulf Stream from Bimini after it has spent the winter spawning. Twenty years ago, the rich waters of the northeast, with vast schools of herring, mackerel, pogies, sand eels, and blue fish, drew the giant bluefin into the Maine coastal areas of Wells, Middle Banks, Stellwagen, and among the lobster holes of Barnstable. Sadly, today they don't come into these waters like the days of old.

In 1980, we spent from June through September on the same piece of bottom on Jeffreys Ledge chasing the same schools of fish every day. The change in where bluefin return to feed may well be due in part to the growth and changes in commercial fishing, particularly related to midwater trawling. Next to seining, there isn't another fishery on the planet that can be so deadly. When the midwater boats started targeting herring and other bluefin food fish inshore, the vast amounts needed to stock these boats came from the same schools that sucked in the bluefin for food.

Fish adapt pretty easily and will change their migration patterns and holding grounds to stay close to their food source. Water temperatures, predators, and fishing pressure can all effect where fish will spend their time. Whatever the reason behind the migration changes in bluefin, you take away their food and a fish that just swam a thousand miles for lunch is damn sure going to go where dinner is served.

Fuel costs for the guy in New Jersey spending four bucks a gallon to run out to the Canyons adds up quickly. Even a few nights at Block

Island or taking a couple of brine bags full of ice and spending an evening offshore involves costs that have been increasing. There's not only a migration in the fish, but in where the boats fish. The Cape Cod guys moving to temporary slips or anchorages in Provincetown to be closer to current offshore fishing is an option. Still, increased fuel costs need to be figured into each new season, and that offshore sashimi is becoming pretty damn expensive to catch.

WALKING THE DOCKS

Kodiak, Alaska

At 7 a.m. on my first morning in Kodiak, I was sitting in the Kodiak Cafe (which has since been torn down) having breakfast and listening in on fishermen's conversations. I learned that the upcoming halibut opening was for two days and prices should be about a dollar a pound.

I couldn't even imagine a halibut opening and had seen less than twenty halibut over ten pounds during my entire time back East. When we did catch one it was sold for shack money, with the fish sold for cash. On some boats the boat took a share and on others shack money was split evenly by the crew. It was a big deal. Now here I was a world away sitting in a cafe hearing about deck loads of these monster flatfish.

After I consumed my $10 meal I was ready to find a position. I never had to look for work like this before, but I'd seen guys back East pounding the docks. I tried to remember what the guys that seemed to find jobs this way said. I couldn't, and decided to wing it.

On the first finger dock I decided to speak to every single boat, telling them who I was, where I was from, and what I knew. If this didn't work, I'd work on Plan B. What that was, I didn't have a clue.

The first dozen salmon seiners I talked to didn't need help. Finally one boat said they did need a guy and one of the crewmembers told me to call the owner, Charlie. I tried about thirty-seven times. He wasn't home. Finally I came to about a 40-foot seiner called the *Lynmark* with a husband and wife team baiting hooks on the back deck. The man's name was Terry and he was in need of someone.

Since I didn't have longlining experience, a deal was struck that I'd go for a half share and if I did the job well they would pay me a full share. I agreed in a heartbeat and ran back to the hotel to grab my gear and boots. The rest of the day was spent baiting hooks until my hands were raw. Late that night I called my folks at 4 a.m. their time to tell them the news.

The next morning I was on my way down to the *Lynmark* when I ran into the crewmember from the first boat that needed someone. He said he spoke to Charlie, and I could go with them. His name was also Terry and I had to let him know I was all set with another job. He knew the *Lynmark* and told me it was a real good sight and the owner was very honest and a good fisherman. He told me to keep in touch and if I was looking for a job later he'd try to help. I thanked him and made my way down the dock for another day of putting pieces of octopus on hooks.

At 6 a.m. the next morning we slid under the ice shoot at Alaska Pacific Seafoods and blew five tons of ice onboard the *Lynmark*. We were on our way to Chiniak Gully for my first halibut opening. In addition to Terry's wife, there was another guy who was supposed to run the roller and be an experienced longliner. He was a tall and rugged quiet man who always had a huge wad of chewing tobacco stuffed in his cheeks. We were ready. The opening was at noon and we still had five hours.

I offered to drive the boat so Terry could lie down. He was probably thinking here's this kid from Maine who has never been in Alaska before, much less outside the boat harbor in Kodiak, and he wants to drive. Like hell. But to me he just smiled and said thanks, that he was fine. I was very pumped and sat back and looked at my watch every five minutes, wishing it was noon.

At noon we laid out about half of our gear in three hours before steaming towards the first buoy set. By 4 p.m. the hooks were coming back onboard with cod, arrowtooth flounder (a junk fish), and some halibut. Fishing was slow for us and by the time we retrieved two sets we had about 1,000 pounds of dressed fish. To me this was unbelievable, but Terry said it really sucked. We tried a few more depths but never really got on the fish and ended with just over 5,000 pounds for the two days the fishery was open.

In those two days we threw back at least 20,000 pounds of cod, dead or alive. After the first few were tossed back into the sea or cut up for fresh bait, I asked Terry why we were doing so. "These are big bucks back East," I yelled up, standing by the roller with a gaff in my hand. "Codfish usually bring in 80¢ to $1.20 a pound."

"Not worth much out here," he said. "We don't want to take up our hole space."

I struggled with this the rest of the day. I came from a fishery where if it came onboard it went in a box. If we couldn't sell it to the market, it went to the lobster men for bait. Throwing back good marketable fish seemed crazy. Why not fill up two times on cod and halibut and steam to town? We could be in town, offloaded, and iced back up in six hours. I held my breath. It was my first introduction to a whole new way of thinking. The North Pacific way of keeping only the good stuff seemed wrong. The attitude that there are a lot of fish, so who cares if you throw some overboard is something I've never been at peace with. Those fish add up to millions of pounds a year.

After delivering the fish to a shoreside plant, we had a day of cleaning and putting gear away. Terry paid me a full share (just under $400) and offered me a job to go salmon fishing in another month. The problem was I needed a job now. I told Terry my situation and he even went as far as trying to find me a temporary job, with no luck. Terry and his wife were leaving the next day for Seattle and I was back where I was a week ago, looking for a job.

KODIAK ISLAND HERRING

I was on my way with my two sea bags back to the Star Motel when Terry, the crewmember from the first boat, drove by. He told me if I wanted to go herring fishing his boat had a spot. I threw my bags in the back of his Bronco and just like that was employed again.

I met the owner/skipper Charlie and soon got the rundown on what we would be doing. Seining for herring around Kodiak Island was (and still is) a unique fishery. From noon of one day to noon the following the fishery is open. Immediately after it closes for twenty-four hours. We worked in a three-boat group called a combine and had a spotter plane which would assist the three boats.

We departed Kodiak the next morning and steamed through Ouzinkie Narrows, Whale Pass, and into Kupreanof Strait. We then turned north up the east side of the island to Afognak Island and into Malina Bay. We arrived about four hours after the opening and met up with our tender and one of the two other boats in the combine. We tied along the side of the tender and I was introduced to the crew on the other boats. The tender was a 60-foot wooden boat called the *Susan* that would be used to transport the catch from the fishing grounds to shoreside processing plants in town.

Soon this beautiful floatplane, a 185 Cessna, buzzed the boat. Our pilot, a real character named David, taxied his plane alongside and jumped out on his float as I grabbed his plane's wing. Dave told the gang he spotted a couple of nice bunches of herring a few bays over and he wanted us to make the move early in the morning with hopes that no one would follow. We had a few beers, ate a big dinner, and played cards. Everyone else turned in around 10 p.m. and I took the first watch at anchor, enjoying the late-night Alaskan sunset.

We pulled away from the *Susan* at 6 a.m. and headed to Viekoda Bay on the south side of Kupreanof Strait, arriving an hour or so before the opening. There were no other seiners other than our three boats around and Dave was the only plane. He told us he could see fish and he'd set us once it was legal to start.

With ten minutes to go, Dave lined us up on what looked to be about ten tons of herring. Terry was in the skiff with the engine running and I was going to be the one to release the quick-release lock on the pelican hook that held the net on Charlie's command. This was great, but I wished I was up on the mast to be able to see this.

As noon ticked off, Dave told Charlie to release and idle slow ahead. The fish were holding tight. As I released the pelican hook, Terry powered the skiff and did a bat turn to anchor his end of the seine. I stepped back and watched the seine creep off the deck, while trying to catch what was being said on the radio.

All of a sudden Charlie put the coals to the engine and cranked the boat around back towards the skiff, making an oval with the net. I snapped Terry's towline up to the tow bridle and then jumped over to help Charlie with the purse line. Ben, our fourth guy, just stood back. It was also his first set.

Charlie said Dave saw the fish spook and they dove, but he seemed to think we had them. As soon as the purse line rings came up we started to stack the seine on deck as it came through the power block. I had the corks and Ben had the leads, and we had about one-third of the seine back onboard when I saw herring jumping. We had 'em. We continued to pull up the seine and finally had the fish in a tight ball.

Charlie estimated the catch to be about twelve tons. Dave landed and taxied over to check the roe content of the fish. We put a tagline on his plane while he and Terry took the skiff to the cork line and netted out a couple of five gallon buckets of fish.

I couldn't see well and had no clue what was going on. I tried to ask Charlie, but was told to shut up and wait. Dave looked up, shook his head, and said, "Green, let 'em go."

What? Those fish weren't green. They were silver. What did he mean let them go? Laughing, Charlie told me that the eggs weren't ripe as we turned the bunch loose.

Over the next four weeks we did catch some nice ripe fish, which sold for about $800 a ton. For the month the three boats caught about 125 tons. The price was split between the boats, tender, and plane, with each group receiving about $20,000. After expenses were taken out, my share was just under $1,600 and I was able to begin a little nest egg to build on. By the time the fishery closed we had traveled all the way around Kodiak Island and visited just about every bay and inlet. It was an enjoyable fishery and a wonderful way to be introduced to the island.

During the off time between openings I was able to do some sport fishing and flying with Dave, and also saw my first brown bear track. I was convinced it belonged to a bigfoot, not a bear.

We made it back to Kodiak on July 1 to change seines and do a little work for the salmon season. Red (sockeye) salmon season had already started and we were in a rush to get the boat rigged up. Not too rushed, though. We decided to stay in for the fourth of July. After two nights of heavy drinking at the Beachcomber Bar, I was ready to experience a Kodiak salmon season.

Reds, Humpies, and Chums

I'd yet to lay eyes on a Pacific salmon, but now I was going to make a living catching them. We departed Kodiak on the morning of July 5, 1985, with all four of us feeling the results of a hard fourth of July weekend. Our destination was Wide Bay on the mainland of the Alaska Peninsula for a red opening scheduled for the next day.

We came out of Kupreanof Strait and headed across Shelikof Strait. The mainland before now had been distant peaks. As we got closer I could start to see the vastness of this country. The mountains were huge and the snow covered peaks majestic. I was in awe.

The next morning we got in line with five other seiners. This was something totally new to me—actually waiting your turn to fish. We were the third boat in line. I was on the flying bridge with Charlie and he explained what we were going to do as we watched the first boat make the noon opening set.

The boat laid out his seine net, which had a hook on one end that was attached to the seiner. A skiff set the other end of the seine, using power to keep it straight. The hook was held for around twenty minutes and we soon saw some salmon jumping along the net's corks.

As soon as the seiner and the skiff started to come together, the second seiner in line laid out his net to take the first boat's place. The fish were running down this beach heading God knows where and we were intercepting them. I was amazed to see a group of fishermen all working together and taking turns. I could see groups up and down the beach and off the cape all doing the same thing. Gentlemen fishermen. Wow. What a concept.

I watched the first guy purse up. He had about one hundred or so fish and I thought that was pretty good for a half hour's work. Charlie seemed bummed. He was hoping for more.

Terry had the skiff up and running and Charlie told me to stand by the release. As the second boat started to close up, I released Terry's skiff with a short pull on the pelican hook and he laid the seine out behind us. We formed our hook, which keeps the fish milling down the length of the seine and keeps the fish from escaping at the ends. We also used plunging to keep the fish from going out the ends. This is done by using a long pole with a cup attached to the end. The pole is forced into the water and the cup creates a loud pop with a good healthy supply of bubbles, scaring the salmon away from the end of the seine. Plunging is done onboard the seiner and also on the skiff. I quickly became an expert plunger—the one who scares the salmon.

I kept a strong eye out for jumpers along the corks and was soon rewarded with a jumper. Then another. Soon the seine seemed alive with leaping fish. Charlie told Terry to start the close. As Terry came alongside, I handed off his end of the seine to Ben and hooked up his towline to the bridle as Charlie started the purse.

We got the purse rings up and the seine was soon coming through the power block that hangs off the boom and takes the net onboard where it is stacked. The salmon seine was longer and deeper than the one we used for herring and I soon found it was a lot more difficult to stack. I managed to keep up to Charlie's fast pace with the block and a somewhat decent cork job was accomplished.

Charlie had the moneybag, the heavy mesh end where the fish end up. The moneybag is pursed up next to the boat and is the last part of the seine to come aboard. He told me to get the brailer, a big fish net used as a scoop to bring fish onboard, while we had them. We brailed aboard two lifts before he said we could roll the rest onboard with the winch. We soon had the full load of around 500 fish (approximately 2,000 pounds) onboard and in the hole. At $1.50 pound, we had just made $3,000. I thought for sure we were going to be rich.

Soon I was greatly disappointed. After that first good set the most reds we caught those next three days were about twenty-five fish a set. All the boats were choking the fish off and the fish started to move offshore. The cape seiners with bigger boats and deeper seines started to do well as the smaller boats began to split the smaller piece of the fish pie.

Red season was slow for us, but when humpies (pink salmon) started to run we did much better. Terry quit and I got the skiff job. I thought this was way cool and it was a lot more fun working from the skiff. There was very little waiting in line and we fished inside of bays and caught lots of fish.

One memorable day was at the Kitoi Bay fish hatchery on Afognak Island. The humpies, a few reds, and dogs (chum salmon) were still coming back to the stream there, and the hatchery already had enough eggs and had met their escapement quota. It was wide open with no markers, which meant we could fish anywhere, and the fish were thick. Really thick. We were one of three boats that morning and we laid out the first set in the mouth of the stream in front of the hatchery's dock.

We managed to choke off the whole stream mouth and it wasn't long before fish were jumping all along the cork line. My end of the seine was dragged by the skiff right to the beach where I tied the skiff to a big tree. The fish weren't getting out my end.

Since the other two boats weren't waiting for us, we held our hook for about an hour. When we closed and pursed up, the seine was full of jumping salmon. We ended up brailing for four or five hours and had over 12,000 pounds for our effort.

We steamed right for the tender and were pumped dry before returning to the stream at 4 p.m. to try again. There were still no other boats and we laid the seine out again, repeating the first set. With two sets and two boatloads of salmon we yielded over 24,000 pounds of humpies, dogs, and a few reds and silvers. We fished until around 1 a.m., becoming tired but extremely happy.

The next morning there were about a dozen more boats in the little bay and the big show was over. We went to town (Kodiak) that night to re-group and deliver the day's fish directly to the plant and save the tender fee.

This would be the last time I would fish commercially for salmon. Although I have very little actual experience, I have a deep respect for the people who make their living salmon fishing in Alaska. There are many variables today, which make this fishery a huge gamble for the fishermen and their families. Salmon fishing is seasonal with a very short window when salmon can be harvested. The Alaska Department of Fish and Game must let a certain percentage of fish (called escapement) reach the spawning grounds before any fish can be caught commercially. If the run is weak, there may not be any openings.

Sport fishing versus commercial creates a controversy in some areas such as Cook Inlet regarding who should have the rights to the fish. It has become a larger and larger issue in some parts of Alaska. In addition, market fluctuations with farm-raised Atlantic salmon now taking a large piece of the pie has sent the price for wild Alaskan salmon plummeting.

Traditional salmon fishermen seem to be backed against the wall these days. I'd hate to think that this fantastic way of life could fade away. In 1985, the Bristol Bay fishery was the largest in the state. By

2002 it was all but dead. A couple of bad returns, prices at a fraction of what they were in 1985, and the huge increase of farm-raised salmon have all but destroyed this once incredible, competitive fishery. It is just one more example of what is happening to each and every one of our country's commercial fisheries.

GRANDPA BURCH

After offloading late that night, we moved the boat back to the Kodiak small boat harbor early the next morning in anticipation of taking the day off. As we went by the harbor breakwater I noticed a trawler tied up to the first finger on the very end of the dock. It was an old Southern-style 86-foot Bender Gulf boat that looked old and tired. She was battered and worn with her white paint streaked with rust. She had two big net reels, a beefy gallest frame, and strong heavy rigging. I was drawn to this boat and could not take my eyes off it as we went by, probably because it was the second trawler I had seen in four months.

When we finished our work and tied up the seiner, Charlie let me borrow the skiff for the day. I pulled up to that old dragger to get a closer look and noticed an old man on deck. I tied the skiff to the rail and asked the old timer if I could come aboard. When this man looked at me I was a little taken back and shocked. He had only one eye, a mouth full of chewing tobacco, and was bald as a cod.

With a smile that reached from ear to ear and a booming voice, he beckoned me aboard. I introduced myself, told him where I was from and what I was doing in Kodiak, and told him that something about his boat drew me to it. I talked for four or five minutes and this old man just smiled and never said a word. Finally he reached over, shook my hand and said his name was Oral but the whole town knew him as

Grandpa Burch. It seemed so natural and I said, "Grandpa, I'm glad to meet you." I called him Grandpa from that day on.

I received the grand tour of the *Dawn* that day. He told me he was retired from fishing but kept his one good eye on his two boats—the *Dawn* and the *Dusk*. The *Dawn* was fishing with the Koreans in the Bering Sea Joint Venture (JV) foreign fishing program. The captain had been out for six months, had enough, and drove the boat back to Kodiak and quit. He was someone who fished with Oral for fifteen years, but Grandpa didn't seem too upset.

Grandpa told me the skipper of his other boat was going to let one of his guys take the *Dusk* and he was flying in from Dutch Harbor. They were going to do a little work to the boat, re-crew it, and send it back out west to the Bering Sea. I made up my mind then and there I was going to the Bering Sea on that boat. Oral took me out for lunch and then up to meet his brother, Al, at the Alaska Draggers Association office in Kodiak. I didn't even know such a place existed, probably because I had been either out on the water or at the Beachcomber's Bar for the past four months.

Al was like the difference between the names of his boats *Dawn* and *Dusk*. Oral was a hard looking, old time fisherman. Al was an office-type politician with soft hands and a mild voice. Al told me the background of the Alaska Draggers Association and a little about the trawl fisheries in the state, while Oral waited patiently.

In the mid-1980s, there was very little shore-based trawling around Kodiak Island. The only boat was the *Royal Baron*, which delivered cod to one of the Moonie plants (run by the Reverend Sun Myung Moon's Unification Church), and this was limited because the salmon season kept all the plants busy.

I told the two Burch brothers that I wanted a job but was salmon fishing with a local guy and didn't feel right about quitting on him. Oral told me the boat wouldn't be ready to go for a couple of weeks and I could give a two-week notice. They promised to hold the job for me and I signed on as the web man, a West Coast term for twine man. I would be the crewmember in charge of the net upkeep onboard the *Dawn* for the remainder of the JV season.

That night I told Charlie and was he ever angry. I was the second skiff man he lost that summer. After finishing out my two weeks with him, Oral chartered a floatplane to pick me up from the fishing grounds and take me back to Kodiak two days before we were set to head west.

The captain of the *Dawn* was Rick Nelson, who had transferred from the *Dusk*. Rick had spent about all of his adult life working for the Burch brothers and is what you'd call a lifer. The rest of the crew included our engineer, Dave, a Kodiak native; John, our cook, who was a friend of Rick's from Anchorage; and me. In addition to being the web man, I was also the deck boss.

I was the last of the crew to show and the guys had the boat loaded and ready to go. We weren't scheduled to leave for a couple of days, but since we were ahead of schedule the old man began throwing the lines, kicking us out of town. We were bound for the Bering Sea. I think he was worried, correctly so, that we'd hit the bars if we had too much free time on our hands. Instead, we took the bar with us, with pallets of beer and enough pot to keep Bob Marley stoned for a year.

The trawl deck was mounded with gear. While we headed out in protective waters we popped the main hatch and stored the spare nets, cookie gear, bare wire section, web, and transfer cables. By the time we were in Shelikof Strait on the north side of Kodiak Island, the deck was secure and somewhat organized.

The gear was completely foreign to me and totally different from anything we used back East. It was much bigger and heavier, and the trawl doors were huge and looked like a pair of wings off a small plane. I learned that they were called Super Vs and were the new hot item.

Over the next few years I developed a love/hate relationship with these hot items. Eventually I leaned all the way to the hate end of the spectrum of the Super Vs and refused to have a set onboard vessels I later ran.

The trawl net had rib lines the size of my wrist to hold them in and the ground gear had 15-fathom shots of 3/4-inch cookie gear, something we could never afford to use in Maine. Cookie gear consisted of a six-strand cable with rubber disks that filled the entire length of the cable to protect it from wear and tear as it is towed across the bottom. We had two net reels full of cookie gear and the spare shots took up a whole pen in the fish hole. Bails of twine (web) were stacked three deep. It seemed to me that we were a floating twine shop.

The ride to Dutch Harbor took three days. Along the way, I saw the Shumigan Islands southwest of the Alaska Peninsula for the first time, as well as the eastern islands of the Aleutian chain and the Bering Sea. When we arrived on the early morning of August 9, 1985 (my twenty-third birthday), the harbor was layered in a heavy fog.

Once the fog lifted, I was surprised at its size and how modern the port was in such a remote location, even though the entire island of Unalaska still didn't have a paved road. And the boats. I'd never seen anything like the trawlers that were tied to various docks. I learned from Rick that most were Marcos (a Seattle-built fishing trawler) and were over 100 feet long. They looked huge and sleek, and were beautifully designed.

We pulled into Petro Marine to top off our fuel tanks and Rick made some phone calls. Before I knew it, we were on our way to meet our mothership to pick up a codend (the back end of the net used in trawling where the fish collect) and to start fishing. It was a brief touchdown that left a lasting memory.

Dutch Harbor, commonly called Dutch, would become like a second home to me in my Alaskan fishing career. Over the years I watched this remote commercial fishing port in the middle of the Aleutian Islands develop beyond my wildest expectations, with a four star hotel, paved roads (at least some), a medical clinic, an excellent school with special programs in fisheries science, a fine library, and a top-notch community center. It became a place where some families chose by preference to raise their kids. The boomtown nature of Dutch Harbor hung on for years, as did its tough reputation. At its heart, however, was the cooperative spirit that ultimately prevailed in making an exceptional community built by a unique breed of rugged Alaskans.

There was a saying among women working at one fish plant that went, "Don't worry gals, when you return to the lower 48 you will be ugly again." They knew it, but enjoyed their time there. With limited competition, men took the time to see their inner beauty for the sake of female companionship. In a strange way, that's also what happens aboard fishing vessels when we're out at sea for any length of time and women are onboard.

Dutch Harbor continues to attract a diverse collection of people from all walks of life, and its economy continues to be based largely on fishing. As a community, it stands strong and has become a classic fishing village. The people who have chosen to call this cold, windswept Aleutian Island home have built a foundation that many communities much closer to everyday amenities can only aspire to.

JOINT VENTURE FISHING DAYS

Trawling With Foreign Vessels

The following day, we met up with our mothership, *Shin Yang Ho*, a huge 350-foot black and white stern trawler from South Korea, who met us at sea to deliver an empty codend. This was the key to delivering fish to them. The mesh bag would zip on the end of our trawling net. Once full of fish, it was transferred back to the mothership.

Rick maneuvered behind the mothership and a buoy was trailed out behind the gigantic vessel on a very long heavy line. We grappled the buoy aboard and hooked the line to our aft net reel. When Rick told the mothership we had hold of the trailing end, they slid the codend down their ramp with a big cluster of buoys to float the bag. We wound up the slack line and began to reel in the empty codend. It was huge and easily as long as our deck. I couldn't tell exactly how big it was because we only brought the mouth of the bag onboard, leaving the rest trailing behind us. We then zippered the codend to our lengthening piece, consisting of an extension piece tapered from the main body of the net to the aft section, using one-inch shackles to attach the rib lines together. This process took over an hour and Rick told us by the end of the week we better have it down to 20 minutes.

Our target species was yellowfin sole. The mothership had to leave to take a delivery from our partner boat, the *Mardel Norte*, which was about eight miles away, so we set out in their direction. The doors (those wonderful Super Vs) spread like no other door I'd ever seen. I estimated the spread was an incredible 400 feet wide.

We made a three-hour tow before hauling back the net and preparing it for delivery to our mothership. After the doors came up, we wound in 100 fathoms of ground gear and started to bring the codend onboard. There were some flatfish gilled in the body of the net and a few in the lengthening piece. The majority of the codend was well below the ramp and we couldn't tell how much was in the bag. We choked off the codend and hooked up a four-bridle setup to the rib lines, which were attached to the buoy bags and the transfer line used to retrieve the empty net. The figure eight was placed into our pelican hook with the large 1-1/2-inch cable. One end was attached to the end of the figure eight and the other end of this cable was snaked around the outside of the boat on the starboard side to midship, where the power block was located. We were ready to transfer.

The mothership came to our starboard side trailing a huge two-inch steel cable hawser behind it. On the spliced end of the hawser there was a smaller diameter tag line attached with a small buoy. We grappled this up and pulled it onboard with the power block. A huge shackle was hanging from the hawser and we attached it to the transfer cable. We coiled up the tag line, threw everything out and ran to the stern. We hit the release on the pelican hook with a sledgehammer, and the codend was released.

As the mothership hauled in the hawser and the codend on their ramp, we all went to the bow to watch. The bag was half full when it went up the ramp, yet it was the most fish I'd ever seen in a single tow. The JV representative gave us a hail weight of 18 metric tons gross weight. This was almost 40,000 pounds of fish—the equivalent of what we would deliver on a seven-day trip for sole on the East Coast.

Fishing and my life back in Maine were gradually being replaced by this newfound wonder, Alaska, which was proving to have the richest fishing waters in the world.

We delivered an average of 50 metric tons a day to the *Shin Yang Ho*, even though we picked up two more catcher boats and had a limited market for what we could deliver. The yellowfin sole sold for $140 a ton, with an average boat gross of $7,000 a day. My 9 percent crew share earned an average of $630 a day—by far the most money I'd ever made.

We stayed out until September 18, before heading back to Dutch Harbor for fuel and food. Our Dutch refit was like a pit stop: 20,000 gallons of fuel, $3,500 in groceries, topping off the freshwater tanks, phone calls, and then back to the fishing grounds in less than twenty-four hours. At over $600 a day in earnings, this was fine by me.

By the first of October the weather was getting bad and fishing began to drop off. We were catching only two or three tons an hour and towing all the time. On October 20, the venture was called a conclusion and we began our way back to Kodiak. When we received our final crew shares at the end of the month, I had made $26,000 for 2-1/2 months of fishing. I called my dad and told him I was never going to leave. Alaska was my new home.

We took about a week to rig the boat over to shore-based fishing. Now the fish we caught would be delivered to shoreside plants rather than motherships at sea. The old captain Gary was back and Rick was going on vacation. He had spent ten solid months fishing in the Bering Sea and was desperate for a break.

I fished with Gary until the 1st of December, shore-basing for cod and selling them to the Moonie plant for a dime a pound. I made a couple more thousand dollars and then decided it was time for me to take a break also. Taking Rick's lead, I headed to Hawaii for Christmas.

I smoked a lot of pot, drank buckets full of fluff drinks, spent a huge portion of my hard-earned money on loose women only too eager to help spend the cash, and in three short weeks flew back to Alaska to catch my breath.

I arrived back in Kodiak on December 28, 1986, to find that Gary had quit again. This time he decided to take a job on shore at a new plant in town. The Burch brothers were without a captain for the *Dawn* and with the JV season coming up, they were in a hell of a bind.

I told Oral that I could run the boat. I felt confident that I could do the job and asked him to give me a chance. He said he'd have to talk to Al and headed towards the Alaska Draggers Association office. I waited about ten minutes, pacing the wheelhouse of the *Dawn*, and then ran for the nearest phone and called the office. Oral answered and told me they were discussing it. I told Oral that if he'd give me a chance, I'd make him proud and would work very hard.

He told me right then and there that I could run the boat. I heard him tell Al, "We're going to take a chance with the kid." I'll never forget those few words. I had my shot.

Our market was with Profish, selling to the Koreans. *P. Yang Ho* was going to be my mothership and I'd have one other catcher boat to split the market with. We were going to start the year trawling midwater for pollock.

I had never even seen a midwater net, let alone caught fish with one. I'd have to wing it. After all, this was still trawling. How hard could it be? I was soon to find out, and went through a huge learning curve those first two months.

We had a month of boat work replacing some destroyed steel in the stern, rebuilding the generator, going over the gear, and loading the boat. With the boat finally ready, I was hoping for the best, but was also scared shitless. We departed February 1 for Dutch Harbor.

My crew was all new. Of the four of us, Don was the only one that had any midwater experience. We arrived in Dutch on February 3, took on fuel, and had a scrambler radio installed to talk in private with our mothership and other boats.

We met up with *P. Yang Ho* February 5 on a flat calm morning. Matt, my American JV representative onboard the *P. Yang Ho*, told me the fleet consisting of close to 200 boats was fishing off Bogoslof Island and that the fish were deep but had good roe content. When I picked up the codend we'd be using, it was a 70-ton monster longer than the boat. And to think before I had thought sole bags were large. Alaska fishing just kept getting larger and larger in terms of gear and equipment.

About twelve miles from the fleet, I started to pick up targets. The next three days were complete hell. I watched catcher boats deliver codends that looked like they were the size of nuclear submarines. There was mass activity within this fleet and money beyond my comprehension was being made. The biomass of fish stretched twenty square miles. The top of the school was so thick and solid it read on the color sounder fishfinder as being the sea bottom.

As other boats, crews, and their captains were becoming rich, I was totally screwed up. I couldn't figure out the ancient wet paper machine that Furuno called a net recorder. It consisted of a headrope transducer that sent a picture of the net's opening, including where the net is in the water and where fish are in relation to the net. You pretty much need this vital piece of information to catch any fish with a midwater net. I didn't have a clue how to read it.

On the second day I crossed the doors that keep the net open and towed the net like that for three hours. The gear came back so tangled up we had to cut the main wires and backstraps with a torch to be able to wind up the twisted net, which looked like a three-foot-thick hawser, onto the net reel. I was defeated and had no business being where I was. I was ready to head back to Dutch and tell Gramps I was in over my head. The crew was totally disgusted and wouldn't even speak to me.

What happened next saved me from losing my job and probably my career. The captain of the *P. Yang Ho* told me to come alongside and his crew would help me untangle my net and he would help me understand the gear and fishery.

We tied alongside and this man's crew took my net and doors aboard their ship. Thirty Koreans untangled my net, which was almost destroyed, and rebuilt it completely. A midwater net is complicated and this was no small task. They even re-spliced my backstraps.

The process took twenty-four hours, during which time the ship didn't take any deliveries. I have no idea how much this cost the ship, but their deliveries averaged about 500 metric tons of fish a day. The boats at this time were roe stripping, taking only the roe from the pollock, which is very valuable. I remember being offshore Bogoslof Island and seeing mile-size patches of pollock carcasses. The seabirds would turn the water surface into a living black mass. Seeing this further hardened me as I saw yet another wasteful practice being considered acceptable at that time. Roe stripping was outlawed in the early 1990s, although boats continued to harvest roe as one part of the total product. Today it sells for over $5 a pound, while the price of pollock filets hovers between $1 to $2 a pound.

The captain spoke broken English but still spent the entire time teaching me how to read the old Furuno 700 wet paper machine. He also explained how to set the net, how to get the net below the school, and basically how to catch pollock.

I never paid more attention to what I was being told than at that time. I took notes, asked a million questions, and eventually left his boat with some kind of a grip of what to do. This man saved a young man who was about to lose it all, and I owe more to him than I can ever repay.

The next four weeks we caught fish, made 70-ton deliveries, and even learned to enjoy midwater fishing. We were probably the low boat in the whole venture, but we survived and stocked a couple hundred thousand dollars in the bank. I learned a lesson to never give up in fishing, no matter how bad it seems to be.

The quality of the roe started to drop the first part of March and we were one of the first boats to switch to sole fishing. We steamed to Dutch on March 2 and changed over to bottom gear. Although the *Dawn* was never really set up well for midwatering, she was very much so for sole fishing and I knew quite a bit more about this fishery in comparison. It was time to make up for being the lowest producer in the midwater fishery that winter.

Sole Fishing

The sole bags the *P. Yang Ho* had were cut down pollock bags that held about 50 metric tons. This was just about twice the size of the bags we had used the previous fall. I was more than a little concerned when we received our first empty one outside Dutch. I asked the captain where we should start and he told me the only other boat that was sole fishing was doing well in Zone 1 at latitude 56°30' north, longitude 164°00' west, so that's where we started.

The other boat was the *Pelagois*, a huge 140-foot combination trawler/crabber with an aft wheelhouse. It was owned and operated by an old Norwegian named Earling. Earling would entertain me with countless stories on the VHF radio for hours, even though it would be months before I would ever meet him face to face. He was in his late-seventies and I felt like I knew him the first time I spoke to him.

Earling told me how one night while towing with a huge fleet of pollock boats he wanted ice cream. He left the wheelhouse and went to the walk-in freezer in the bow of the boat to get it. Before he realized it, the door locked behind him. Now picture this old man being the only guy awake onboard and locked in a freezer in the bow of his boat while towing among a fleet. He looked around the freezer for something to beat the door down with. The largest object he could find was a leg of lamb. An hour later he was out and the freezer door was a battered piece of old twisted metal. He ate what remained of the lamb the next day.

Another one of his stories took place during World War II when he was a boy of eighteen in Norway. Earling joined the Navy and was a private loading a freighter in a small harbor when the Germans attacked the town, bombing the boats and piers. The officers of the freighter were on leave and no one could move the boat. The vessel's engineer was frantically trying to find someone capable of operating a 500-foot boat. Young Earling volunteered and ended up saving the ship. The Norwegian Navy eventually made him a captain.

My favorite Earling story is when he was home in Seattle. He heard a knock on the door and found it was some young people who belonged to Greenpeace, asking for a donation. They mentioned something about Norwegian whaling and Earling invited them into his home and made them tea as he got out some of his old scrapbooks. You see, at one time Earling was a whaler and he had a lot of pictures to show these young people. The Greenpeace gang didn't get a donation, but I'm sure they received an education and left Earling's house a little pale.

When we arrived at the fishing grounds Earling told me he was catching about 20 metric tons a tow, but was also catching a lot of derelict crab pots. We caught three on our first tow. Crabbers tend to lose a lot of pots, with pots ranging in size from 6' x 3' x 6' to 8-footers and do a lot of damage to our nets. The number of pots that litter areas of the Bering Sea is incredible. I have some designated crab pot dumps in my wreck book that have over 100 pots.

I ended up trying to make the same tow over and over, slowly widening out and extending on the ends to stay clear of the pots. When the fishing slacked off we would move and clear out another tow. Even so, I caught thirty pots that first week and did a ton of damage. Still, I averaged 100 metric tons of payfish a day, which meant about $2,000 into my pocket each time.

The fleet showed up the following week and everyone agreed to put the pots on the corner numbers, such as latitude 56°00' north, longitude 164°00' west. We slowly managed to clear pots out the area, but it also meant over one hundred catcher boats cleared out the fish too. We were back in search mode.

Rick Nelson on the *Dusk* was fishing for the Russians in the JV program and had some good fishing north of us, so we headed his direction on March 18. I was about thirty miles from the Russian fleet when we went over a huge patch of fish sign. It was a blue haze on the color sounder and two fathoms thick. I thought it had to be some sort of feed, but decided to try a tow through it. We set out on the edge of the sign and within five minutes of getting the gear on the bottom my doors came right together and the boat slowed down to almost no forward motion, from 3.4 knots to 1 knot over the bottom. All I could think about was I had just driven into someone's crab pot dump and must have destroyed the net.

We were lucky. The day was flat calm. The sign had been yellowfin after all, and boy did we have them. There were yellowfin sole gilled everywhere, and we could only get the net up to the leg wires and had to strap it aboard. The codend wasn't full because the small four-seam net we were towing couldn't handle such a huge volume and this was a good thing. It would have been overkill for the boat. Instead, the net shut down from the total weight before we could fill the codend. Still, we delivered 42 metric tons of pure yellowfin (over 92,500 pounds).

By the time we went to transfer the codend, it was so heavy that when the pelican hook was released, the release of the heavy weight from the stern lifted the back of the boat up two feet into the air and we shot ahead with a burst of speed.

Delivering these heavy sole bags was a challenge for the crew. Unlike pollock codends that float behind the boat due to air-filled swim bladders in the fish, the sole bags full of bottomfish would hang straight up and down, causing dead weight to hang off the stern ramp.

Steering was very sluggish and you had to have Mom (the mothership) make a slow close approach and lay her hawser as close as possible. The crew had to get the transfer cable hooked up as quickly as possible and released onto the hawser so we could get our boat clear.

We delivered three more bags like that first one, ending the day with 170 metric tons of payfish. The mothership was plugged up for twenty-four hours. That day I learned another very important lesson—to shut up on the radio. I was so excited about this massive body of fish I had to tell some of my fishing friends about it. They told their friends, and friends told their friends. The next day the Japanese, Russian, and Korean fleets all arrived to share the bounty. Before long the school was broken up and we were in search mode again.

This went on for the next three weeks. We would find a body of fish, get one or two good days, then be back to scratch fishing and searching for the next motherlode. The boat had a $270,000 gross that March, but then fell to just over $100,000 gross in April due to bad weather.

Despite my initials setbacks, for my first three months of running a boat in Alaska I had personally made about $60,000. I sent large sums of money to my father to hold because I didn't trust myself. It was a good thing, because he made sure I paid my taxes. A twenty-three-year-old kid with that much money doesn't always think of paying taxes and more than one fisherman has gotten into trouble with the IRS.

Fishing in late spring and early summer was much slower. The big shot was over and I quickly learned about seasonal changes in the Alaskan fishing industry. By late May almost every species of fish in the Bering Sea and Gulf of Alaska have finished spawning. The males and females are rail thin and disperse to recover. To a fisherman, this means the fish are poor quality and hard to catch because they are not grouped up.

A lot of boats went to fish Atka mackerel in the Aleutian Island chain, but we didn't have the horsepower or range and decided to stay with the smaller boats fishing sole from mid-April to mid-June. We were put into a group of catchers with four boats to one mothership, with a limited market of about 35 tons a day. We averaged $100,000 a month in boat stock, which was still about $7–10,000 for a crew share.

The last shot occurred in mid-June, when fish began to show in Togiak, Bristol Bay, to spawn. Bristol Bay is a shallow water bay that has an incredible herring fishery. Lots of herring come in to spawn, followed by populations of yellowfin sole. These bodies of herring and yellowfin are the only exceptions to all the other Bering Sea fish being finished with spawning by May.

I don't know who found yellowfin sole in Bristol Bay originally, but whoever did must have been extremely shocked. Off of Cape Constantine to Hagemeister Island in towards Togiak the water shallows up from the low teens in fathoms (over 70 feet) to three or four fathoms deep (18–24 feet). After the herring spawn and during the Bristol Bay red salmon season, yellowfin sole pour into this bay to spawn. The fish are sometimes found in waters so shallow that you can see your trawl net floats on the surface while towing and the mud cloud from your trawl doors dragging the bottom.

There is an island in this area called Round Island where a large number of male walruses hang out, stacked up on the beaches. Thousands of these animals were at Round Island and there was a two-mile no entry limit around the island in the mid-1980s. (Now it is twelve miles for boats, with the exception of Alaska Natives who are allowed to enter and harvest some of the walruses.)

We would see walruses every day and they didn't seem bothered by us. They seemed curious and interested, rather than threatened. Some guys towed up old fossilized headsets that consisted of whitened skulls with tusks in place. The only one I was lucky enough to get was confiscated by the Coast Guard and is probably on some admiral's wall today. At the time, I was told it was illegal to keep. I have since found this not to be true because it was old and fossilized, not raw ivory.

Bristol Bay was an enjoyable area to fish, with semi-protected waters, great scenery, and wildlife I had only read about before. The Native people were very friendly and one day I had four Natives pull up in a skiff, tie up, and come onboard to visit while we were towing along. We shared a sandwich, they told us stories, and we traded magazines and beer for ivory pieces before they departed to hunt seals and walruses.

There were up to 200 motherships and catcher boats in this bay all at the same time, which was quite a sight. We brought a lot of money into local towns while conducting big crew changes out of Dillingham and Togiak, along with buying groceries and fuel. The people treated us well and we never terrorized the towns and villages, as fishermen sometimes have a reputation of doing.

I remember one tow in early July when I set out near this little island that was nothing more than a really big rock called Black Rock. White Rock would have been more appropriate, since it was covered in bird guano. There wasn't a speck of grass or single plant growing on this rock. Birds of all kinds totally ruled this little island paradise, chasing off invaders, including an occasional walrus or any person brave enough to approach the rock in a skiff. Yes, we tried with a skiff. Good thing we had on full rain gear. We and the skiff were completely covered in bird guano by the time we escaped.

For fishing we would start off about 1/4 mile from this rock in seven fathoms of water and tow towards Round Island, dropping off into 14 fathoms and hugging the two-mile limit north of the island. Once we cleared the border by about a mile we would haul back the net, ending up in 10 fathoms, which is deep enough for a delivery to Mom. Motherships need to be in at least six fathoms of water (36 feet) and had to be three miles from land to be legal to process fish onboard. If we towed the other way we'd have to tow the bag offshore to Mom, which usually took more time than actually catching the fish.

This towing area was a good producer. The rest of the fleet was off the beach of Cape Constantine and I had this little area all to myself for about two weeks until I was discovered by a few of the guys. Soon this area was pounded by other fisherman and fishing was over, but we made a lot of money for quite awhile in this hot spot. A note in my log says that I caught over three million pounds during the month of July, worth just under $200,000. Today, after seven or eight years of no one being able to legally tow there, I often wonder how many fish must be there. The Coast Guard has seized more than one vessel for going inside this boundary and the fines are enormous. Sadness.

The fish in the bay move out of the area just as fast as they arrive. One day we'd be getting good tows and then the next day they were gone. This year it happened in early August and we were back in search mode, grouped back up to three boats and one mothership. A lot of foreign vessels were going directly to fish for pollock in the Donut Hole, an area outside the 200 mile limit in international waters between Alaska and Russia. Boats from all countries are allowed to fish in the Donut Hole and a group who represents all the interested countries regulates it.

We chose not to travel that far and finished the year in early October. I was on the water from early February to mid-October, with a gross income of over $120,000. My tax bill was over $40,000 that year, which still left a good sum for my effort. I bought a new truck, motorcycle, and made a down payment on a duplex in Kodiak. My father helped guide me on making a few investments, but for the most part I blew the rest of the money.

At twenty-four, I had never made any real money before and man, could I go through it. I spent thousands of dollars on helicopter skiing in British Columbia. It was an expensive habit, but when I compare it to what other JV fishermen spent cash on (mostly cocaine), I feel my ski habit was the wiser of the two.

I have some good memories of that November and December skiing and partying with other fisherman, but when I think about it today I could cry. Did I learn my lesson? Hell no. I did it again and again for the next three years, spending money almost as soon as I made it. I thought the big money in fishing was never going to end.

THE RUSSIAN YEARS

Old Boats, Weird Fleet, and Rules

In 1987, the Burch brothers switched us over to the Marine Resources Company (MRC) for a Russian venture in an effort to get both the *Dawn* and *Dusk* fishing the same market. I lasted two years with this outfit but just wasn't cut out to be a fleet boat. This was communist Russia with political officers, hammer and sickle flags, and homemade vodka.

The Russian boats were referred to as BMRTs. At the time I had no idea what that stood for, but believed it meant Big Mother Russian Trawlers. Later I found out it stands for *Bolshoi Morozilni Rybolovny Traler*, which in Russian means a large freezer fishing trawler.

BMRTs were built in the late 1950s through the 1960s and were old archaic rigs with equipment such as old tube radars, mechanical winches, no Lorans for positioning, and old Russian charts that I can't believe worked to catch fish with. The boats were about 270 feet long, weighed around 1500–1800 gross tons, carried eighty to ninety people, and could produce 80–100 metric tons of fish a day. These boats and crews were some of the same vessels that fished the Grand Banks and later the inshore waters of the New England coast before the 200-mile limit went into effect. A good book has been written about this era called *Distant Waters* by William Wagner.

As I got to know them, the Russians were some of the nicest people I've ever met and they were so interested in us. The majority of workers were very poor to our standards, but they were proud people. Their few possessions were precious to them. They loved American products and we gladly gave them Playboys, other girlie magazines, cigarettes, chewing tobacco, plastic flashlights, walkmans, tapes, and batteries. Any time something was given it would disappear inside a jacket with a quick glance at their companions and a sharp eye kept out for where the political officer was.

In return they would give us their cigarettes (which really sucked), Russian fur hats, homemade vodka, and lead bread. Lead bread was heavy dark bread that weighed about five pounds a loaf. I would toast it with butter and have never found any bread that's its equal.

The political officers were always present whenever we would go over for a visit while fueling or doing gear work. We'd try and tie up at least once a month to get together and no one, not even the captain or other officers, were ever at ease with the political officers around. The boats all had an American JV representative onboard who was a fisheries observer for the National Marine Fisheries Service (NMFS). The reps were usually college kids who majored in Russian and could speak it.

The American reps would tell me stories about the political officers. On my main mothership for the next two years, I had the same political officer on the ships *Ms. Shelikova* and *Ms. Grotivie*. I tried to mess with him as much as possible and remembered my fishing friend on another boat, Richard McLellan, once gave this guy *Red Storm Rising* by Tom Clancy. The officer could read and speak English very well and the book really shook him up. We told him it was all true and never to mess with Americans. I thought this was great and the next trip got him a copy of *Hunt for Red October*, also by Clancy. This book angered him and he told me he thought it could never happen.

When Richard and I finished with him after those two years he must have thought American propaganda was out of control. I kept sending him *Soldier of Fortune*, gun magazines, and every war novel I could find and had great fun at the expense of this poor guy.

The MRC catcher boat fleet was made up of smaller 70- to 90-foot trawlers about the size of the *Dawn*. The high horsepower (hp) guys in the fleet had around 1,000 hp. The fleet was very organized with a radio hour every day talking about who was catching what, and where the best fishing was. And there were rules. Codends couldn't be more than 25 tons because they didn't want to break the Russian equipment with monster bags. If you plugged up the mothership you had to call the fleet head representative and he would put you on the outside tow list. Dirty fishing was considered bad—very bad. If you broke one of these rules, the fleet commander would put you on twenty-four hours of no fish time. Kind of like fish jail.

I found the Russian rules asinine and was the fleet rebel for the next two years. I took great pride in delivering big bags with 30–40 tons of fish. I'd bribe my rep with $50 for each outside tow he/she could line me up with on the sly. I'd lie about my position and beg my rep not to tell what I was catching on radio hour. I know I wasn't liked very well and didn't care. I loved it. If I did get shut down, I figured I'd go deliver bags to the Japanese, Koreans, Polish, or Red Chinese, and then tell the Russians, "Great, all right, I can make more money with these other guys anyway. Shut me down for two days, okay?"

One time I received two warnings for delivering bags over 25 tons and got a call from Dema, the head rep. He told me one more time and I wouldn't be allowed to tow for twenty-four hours. I responded there was a Korean boat with their catcher broken down and that I'd volunteer to stop for twenty-four hours because I knew I was bad.

"Or screw it, make it seventy-two hours," I said.

He told me no, no, that they needed the fish, but not to do tows over 25 tons.

"Okay," I told him, and then the next bag was bang, 35 tons. He was angry with me but wouldn't shut me down because he knew I was baiting him. When the Korean mothership's catcher returned from town for repairs I went ahead and restricted my codends back to 25 tons. Losing my outside market forced me to toe the line until my next opportunity came along.

I joke about it, but this was the period in my fishing career where my attitude changed and I became cocky. I could catch fish as well as anyone in my vessel class. I bent the rules as far as I could, trying to see where the limit was.

COD FISHING

We started 1987 fishing for Pacific cod off of Unimak Pass. The whole fleet would start down at the south end of an edge nicknamed the starting gate. At first light about forty boats would line up three or four deep along the edge. The whole gang would make two- to four-hour tows to the northeast, deliver their codends, and then steam back to the starting gate for the next tow, with everyone always towing the same direction.

I was told that fish went in better and there was a better catch rate by towing to the north. I went along with the gang because everyone seemed to do it this way. The cod wouldn't settle down and bunch up until daylight, so we only fished during daylight hours. In January and February, we worked from about 8 a.m. to 6 or 7 p.m., and then we'd drift or anchor up. The wind direction would determine where and if we'd drop the hook (anchor). It was a pretty laid-back fishery, but profitable. The cod were sold for $240 a ton, which was considered a decent price in those days.

Unimak Pass is the first major pass in the Aleutian Islands. False Pass, which occurs before it, is pretty much characteristic of its name. You can make it through False Pass on smaller vessels (I've done so on the *Dawn*) but I would never attempt it with a bigger boat. Even on the *Dawn* we ran aground twice on sandbars and I remember being scared shitless.

The tide that runs through Unimak Pass is substantial and is a notorious weather spot. Big winds with strong tides make this a tough place to fish. My wreck book has pages full of major wrecks and lost gear in the pass. The pass is also where cod come each winter to spawn. These fish show in great numbers in early January and stay grouped up until mid-March. I had fished cod around Kodiak before, but never at a time of year when they bunched up.

This was something totally different, with big 2–3 fathom high bunches whitelining the paper recorder. In a whitelining bunch, the school is so dense that the echo sounder will not read completely through the fish and a white line appears on the machine's readout with what looked like haystacks with clear spots in the center of each stack. Boy did they add up. When we'd run the headrope transducer the bunches would go in great blobs, blocking out the picture completely on the fishfinder screen. Each one of these big schools would contain 2,000–5,000 pounds of cod.

There were about forty JV boats fishing for cod. By 1988, there were over one hundred, with some factory trawlers and shore-based boats joining in. Shore plants began gearing up to process the increasing amount of cod being caught. The fishery was good and we made a lot of money, fishing until mid-March and then switching over to sole.

Today most of the old JV catcher boats deliver to shore plants, although some still deliver codends to factory trawlers. The factory trawler fleet has grown to its market and fishery maximum. In addition, there is a factory and shore-based longlining fleet, and crab boats sometimes fish for cod with pots when not fishing for crab. The changes in fishing for cod almost year-round started putting them under terrific pressure. The big schools of 1987 and 1988 are no more, and the cod don't ever get the opportunity to group up like they did in the past, with little pressure on the fishery.

I took the first part of the year off in 1988 to ski. Gary came back and having two captains and crew to rotate kept everyone from getting burned out. When I returned in mid-February there were a lot more boats. Richard McLellan returned on his boat and became my regular fishing partner. Richard was also from Maine and the two of us got along from the start, pairing up with the same mothership, *Ms. Shelikova,* that spring. I don't think Russia has ever been the same since.

One day in early March it was blowing about 60 knots northeast and the entire JV and shore-based fleet was anchored up in Lost Harbor off of Akutan Island. I was lying next to a big Marko vessel, the *American Eagle,* and he pulled his anchor early the next morning. It was still blowing but the weather was supposed to come down late that night. No one else was moving, but I decided to follow the larger boat out.

The ride across the pass was flat out scary. We tried to keep the *American Eagle* in sight and kept going. Our mothership couldn't believe we went out and soon followed off our side, keeping an eye on us. We arrived at the fishing grounds and somehow were able to set out our net in huge crashing seas, with the wind still blowing 50 knots. I was hoping it would die down by the time I had to haul back the net.

We towed three hours, never seeing the bottom. It was too rough to even get a picture on the sounders. When it was time to haul back, the mothership reluctantly came alongside to windward to try and knock the seas down and shelter us from the weather, which seemed to help.

We managed to deliver 25 tons of banged up cod and by the afternoon the weather came down enough that we were able to get in another delivery before dark. We were the only boat in our fleet to deliver any fish that day and the mothership, *Ms. Shelikova,* thought we were crazy, even though it was very happy to get the fish.

Today I would never go across the pass in that weather, but back then we really didn't know any better. We were either brave, dumb, greedy, or lucky—I don't know which—but at day's end we were all happy and proud.

FISHING THE ICE PACK

The winter of 1988 was very cold, with temperatures as low as -40° F in Anchorage. The ice pack (floating ice) moved down to 56° north that winter, the lowest I've ever seen. We were on the edge of the ice when we shifted over to sole in early March. The sea resembled a frozen ocean and was like a different world.

At the edge of the ice pack the ice is only six to twelve inches thick and breaks easily. As you travel north it gets thicker, harder, and more consistent. When it gets to be about eighteen inches to two feet thick you can stand and walk on it, which my crew discovered to be great fun.

The ice pack moves north when there are warm winds from the south and south when cold winds blow in from the north, northwest or northeast. This can be very frustrating if you're having a good day fishing and then the damn ocean freezes. The nice thing about ice, however, is no matter how hard it blows you can run into the ice, shut down, and let her blow. There's no swell or chop and the seas can't build.

Throughout the month of March into early April we'd either fish the edge of the pack or steam north looking for open patches of water we'd call duck ponds. These patches would be either large open strips for a couple miles or little two-acre ponds. I leaned towards the ponds because the fishing always seemed better there and I could get away from the fleet and be one-on-one with my mothership.

The disadvantage of being by ourselves in a pond with no outside tows to compete with is that sometimes the ponds close up and leave us miles from open water. When this happened, we'd get behind our mothership's stern ramp and let the larger ship break the ice up. We'd pick a direction and off we'd go, looking for more open water.

Later we discovered that if we pulled our main wires into our ramp we could set out and tow this way, but only did this if we couldn't find open water. After we hauled back I'd nose into the ice out of the lane and wait with quite a bit of power on. The prop wash would keep the bag away from the wheel and we'd wait for Mom to open up an area big enough to deliver the bag.

Once again the captain of *Ms. Shelikova* thought we were crazy, but loved the fish. He'd go along with just about all my crazy schemes and was a bit of a rebel himself.

During one blow that April we were getting winds over 100 knots yet the fleet was 30 miles up into the ice, safe and sound. I sat in the wheelhouse watching it blow so hard you couldn't step foot outside, yet the boat didn't move at all. It didn't even seem like we were on a boat. It was more like I'd imagine being at a research site in the Antarctic amidst a frozen landscape in a massive storm. The ice pack was both a curse and a blessing that winter, depending on our situation.

As time went on we became more proficient at the ice game and would get into areas with four or five ponds separated by strips of ice. We'd get Mom to break out lanes connecting these ponds and tow by hopping from one pond to the next through the lanes. We'd try to end up in an area big enough to transfer the codend at the end. If we'd end up in a tight spot we'd just suck the bag up onto the ramp and off we'd go through our lanes to a bigger area. It was bizarre and strange. It seemed the weirder, more crazy ideas we'd come up with, the more fish we'd catch and money we'd make.

One day we were in a large seven to ten mile-long open area that was a mile or so wide and there were five or six other boats in the area. We passed one vessel that was headed towards a bunch of loose drifting flows with 100- to 200-foot sheets of floating ice. He was headed for another open area that was separated by about a half mile of thick pack ice.

We decided to run to the end of the area we were in and to set behind this guy and follow him over to the other pond. He was about 3/4 of a mile in front of us when I got my net and doors down and sucked my main wires into the ramp so they wouldn't catch on the ice. He, on the other hand, started into the pack ice towing along like he was in the wide open ocean. His main wire caught on the ice and he just kept on going.

The next thing I saw were his doors crashing up through the ice, slamming and banging all the way. Then his ground gear and finally his whole net were all being dragged across the top of the ice. He never slowed down and continued to plow his way through. I reached for the microphone two or three times to call him, but was laughing so hard I couldn't have spoken if I had wanted to.

I watched a piece of ice about the size of his boat go into the mouth of his net, ripping, tearing, and shredding its way towards his codend. When he finally made it to open water, his doors fell off the ice into the water, followed by what remained of his net, and off he went without a clue until he hauled back later. My stomach ached from laughing so hard. There are some people who just shouldn't be out fishing.

Another ice incident took place in a relatively small pond about a square mile in size. The surrounding ice was extremely thick (about a meter or so) and the fish were thick. We'd fill 25–30 tons of fish in one pass and then suck the bag onto the ramp, nose the bow of the boat into the ice, and let Mom pound out a delivery path for us.

We were on our third such delivery that day and Mom was slow getting to us because they would pull into the ice to shut down and process the fish after each delivery. I just happened to have my feet up reading a novel while waiting for Mom to come break me out of the ice. Unbeknownst to me, my crew of three was having a football game out on the ice pack. They weren't paying any attention to our mothership heading towards us at 6–8 knots, and it takes a lot more than a duck pond worth of space to stop a 275-foot vessel traveling at that speed.

The Russian captain in very broken English told me over the radio that my crew was very dangerous. I didn't have a clue about what he was trying to tell me. I told him they might be a little messed up, but they were basically good guys.

I didn't see my crew until the same time they saw the mothership bearing down on them. They all started screaming as the mothership's horn blasted and did a hundred yard dash in deck suits and heavy boots that would make the fastest NFL receivers jealous. They made it back in time, but just so. Needless to say, they played their last Bering Sea football game.

By the end of April the ice was fast retreating north. I ended my 2-1/2 month stint and headed for Dutch, where I rotated off and caught the remaining few weeks of ski season. Once again, I spent my earnings.

NEW WATERS

Rip, Tear, and Shred

In June of 1988 I returned to the boat fully rested and looking forward to summer and nice weather. I was also broke after paying taxes and spending vast amounts of cash on whims. I had a new crew with me and off we headed to the Pribilof Islands to team up with my fishing partner, Richard McLellan. This time our JV representative for NMFS was Tracy for the ship *Ms. Grotva*. Before the next three weeks were up, I'd be pretty much kicked out of the Russian venture and Richard would be madly in love with Tracy.

The Russians had sent most of their motherships back to Russia, leaving about six ships to handle twenty-five catcher boats. This put us at a four-to-one ratio, which in fishermen terminology is one tow a day. The rock sole were thick and we were towing about two hours and drifting for twenty. The head rep thought it would be a great idea to pool the fleet's gross available money together and split it between all the boats. I went looking for an outside market.

The lone Japanese mothership, *Oke Bono No. 1*, didn't have a catcher. I grabbed this market so fast I don't think the captain knew he had a catcher until my first bag was going up his ramp. *Oke Bono* could take about 70 metric tons a day, which kept me very happy while I also tried to do my one tow for the Russians and collect $2,500 or so from the pool. On paper it looked really good.

Problems started quite soon, however. The Russians and their catchers all moved north of St. Paul Island in the Pribilof Islands and the Japanese stayed to the south, with about thirty miles separating the fleets. I decided to stay with the Japanese market and literally told the Russians to kiss my ass. They in turn told me to stuff my codends. Meanwhile, Richard didn't care at all and stayed with the Russians. He was infatuated with Tracy and they were married within a year.

We fished rock sole for the next three weeks. The Japanese were really grateful and sent us lots of beer and fine foods. By the first of July, however, fishing was slowing down and I decided, much to Oral Burch's dismay, to return the boat to Kodiak Island and gear up for an August venture with another Japanese group.

Oral met us at the city dock in Kodiak on July 10, helped tie up the boat, and pointed to his truck. Oh no, I thought to myself. I climbed in and proceeded to receive my first butt chewing from a one-eyed, pissed off old man.

Oral stuck out three fingers and said, "One, you were making $10,000 a day and you leave. Are you on drugs?"

Before I could respond he said, "Two, you tell the whole Russian fleet to kiss your ass on the radio. Are you mental?"

At this point I'm kind of shaking and thinking, Christ, what the hell is number three?

"Three, you best make a boatload of money on this Kodiak venture young man. Now let's go up to the house and have lunch. You can tell me about those Russians."

After a couple of weeks of boat work that included engine room maintenance, gear work, and some modifications to the nets, we were ready for the August venture. At this point my total bottom trawling experience around Kodiak Island was about three months and only in a few spots. I was very green when it came to island towing.

Kodiak waters have a lot of shelves, ledges, pinnacles, and hard rocky bottoms. The edges are steep, tides run hard, and currents are strong. It's a tough place to learn. For the next two months the crew and I spent more time mending and repairing destroyed nets than we did fishing. You could say I learned Kodiak dragging the hard way.

Our fleet in Kodiak consisted of ourselves and another catcher boat called the *Topaz*, along with three small 150-foot Japanese catcher/processors with twenty-man crews. These little factory trawlers were very modern, had state of the art electronics and machinery, and could produce 40–50 metric tons a day of finished product. This was a time before factory trawlers had arrived in force to fish Alaska's rich waters and was a period in American fisheries when they were just being heard of. They were not thought of in good terms. Anytime fishermen hear of another guy smoking them on dollars earned, they instantly hate the guy. To make matters worse, the few out fishing were enjoying almost unrestricted access to whatever was worth the most. The factory trawler *Rebecca Irene*, which I later captained in the late 1990s, was said to have made million dollar trips during its first summer in Alaska in 1987—at the hands of a young Maine captain in his twenties.

There were two other catcher boats that were also supposed to be joining us, but they were still in the shipyard in the lower 48. We had the market to ourselves and a great opportunity to make some money. The *Topaz* stayed in the Bering Sea fishing with the Russians for a week longer than me, so I was ready with the *Dawn* before him.

I met the first of the Japanese processor vessels to arrive, the *Ono*, on August 1. It was a Profish vessel with a woman named Jane as their American JV representative. She was always in good spirits and had a friendly voice on the radio that made days at sea a comfort. It's funny how it's the little things you remember about people. I can't remember what Jane looked like, but I'd recognize her voice in a heartbeat.

We picked up a codend and started the venture in Chiniak gully just outside of town, one of a handful of places I knew. Our target species was supposed to be rock sole and we were going to be paid $150 a metric ton (7-1/2¢ a pound). Our first tow came back with everything except rock sole and was mostly pollock. The *Ono* wanted to go look for better percentages of sole and marketable fish and the search began. Almost immediately we started to tear up our gear in the search.

On the southeastern end of Kodiak there is a bank shaped like a horse. The body of the horse has a deep bank and is all sand; making a good towing bottom, but the edges get harder the shallower you go. We found some rock sole at 40 fathoms, but the bottom was very hard and we paid for each tow with lost web from our net. The crew was getting bummed out as we broke out a second 400-pound bail of polynet fiber for repairs after three days of fishing.

I was finally learning how to tow at this location when the *Topaz* arrived. Mark, the skipper, wanted to go where he had fished the summer before, so we headed off on an eighteen-hour steam to Chirikof Island. We fished a total of four days and delivered about 100 metric tons of sole and 50 metric tons of cod. In the process we took out four bellies and associated panels from our nets and two nets no longer had wings, the closest extended panels of web in a net. We finally gave up on wings because we'd lose them every tow.

Chirikof Island was another place I didn't have a clue about. The edge is extremely steep and you could be towing in 50 fathoms with the guy next to you a boat length away towing in 60 fathoms. Picture a ski run with about a thirty-degree pitch. It was difficult to plot the edge for reference points. I'd start setting out my net in 40 fathoms and by the time my gear was on the bottom I'd be off the edge in 70 fathoms. Mark, however, already had the information plotted from previous years and began filling the *Ono* and a second mothership with codends stuffed with cod and rock sole, at over 30 metric tons each.

On top of having difficulty learning the edge, the area was an old king crab fishing area from the 1970s and 1980s and there were literally hundreds of lost pots littering the bottom. On average I caught five or six crab pots a day, causing even more damage to my nets.

Somehow we managed to put some fish aboard the motherships, but Mark was out-fishing me two or three to one. I was going mental and was always in a bad mood as I continued to tear up gear, even though I tried hard not to. After about four or five days of Mark waxing me, I hooked up with a third mothership that arrived and left Mark with the first two to fill. I steamed thirty miles north just to get away and try somewhere new.

I looked the chart over and found a spot that looked really fishy and delivered a full bag after the first pass. For the second tow I extended it a little to the north. Even though I didn't tow more than ten minutes past my old track, I hung up solid on the bottom. When we started the winches the boat began to slide back over the top of the gear. What I hoped was a ball of cod turned out to be a wreck. Just like that, I lost the first net of my career.

The mothership spent eight hours trying to grapple the net off the wreck. They got a piece of web and busted loose some floats, but in the end they hung the grapple up solid and parted their main wire. The grapple also became history.

We hooked up our spare net and headed back towards the *Topaz*, fishing alongside Mark for another week before deciding to head to Kodiak for fuel, groceries, and to re-supply our gear inventory. I needed more bails of web and seizing twine. Two more catcher boats were due to join us and I needed to be ready. In three weeks the total tonnage I delivered was about 600 tons compared to Mark's 1,200 tons. In addition, I had lost one net, almost 1,200 pounds of 4 mm poly web, 200–300 pounds of mending and seizing twine, and I had a tired and depressed crew.

After re-supplying we departed Kodiak the next morning with a third catcher boat, *Ocean Hope*, joining us. A fourth boat, *Little Bear*, was on its way from California. The Moonies owned *Ocean Hope* and a guy named Dana was running it. The three boats were now one-on-one with the motherships and we headed for Portlock Bank, another place I'd never towed before. We caught quite a few cod during the next two days but our bycatch numbers of prohibited halibut, which we were required to release, was higher than acceptable and would close down the fishery if we weren't careful. Mark and I moved to another area called Barnabas Gully, but Dana stayed.

We fished four more days at Barnabas Gully when we received word that our venture had met the halibut quota. The *Ocean Hope* caught 75 percent of our group's allowable percentage of halibut and had shut us down. I've had this thing about the Moonies ever since. A summer venture that should have lasted into the fall was over in five weeks. The *Little Bear* never made it in time and didn't even get to set their net.

We talked Oral into letting us take the boat to the shipyard and do a complete refit inside and out. A little shipyard in Blaine, Washington, was picked to do the haul out. It was the first time the *Dawn* would leave the state of Alaska since it was built in 1971.

By the first of September I was on my way to the West Indies for three months of sunshine, sailing, and exploring the Caribbean. Lots of money to spend always leads to instant friends and misadventures, which is another story in itself. When I returned from the islands in late November, I flew into Seattle and headed to the shipyard.

The refit of *Dawn* was near completion and after ten weeks in the yard the old sled was actually looking good. The hull was freshly painted and the house had been completely redone, with rewiring, rebuilt machinery, and a rebuilt engine. I was impressed. By the second week of December we were on our way up the Inside Passage and headed home to Kodiak.

The Inside Passage is a water route that takes you from Washington to Southeast Alaska inside protected waters. It starts in the San Juan Islands in northern Washington and heads up through Canada on the east side of Vancouver Island to Prince Rupert before crossing the border into Southeast Alaska. There are lots of small coastal villages and towns and the area is surrounded by huge tracks of forests.

This was my first trip through the inside and we took our time, stopping off at many of the towns and exploring the area. We took eight days to make the trip, even though it can be done in four. When we tried to make it out though Icy Strait into the Gulf of Alaska, it was blowing so hard we were forced to anchor up in a bay and wait out the weather. We spent another three days anchored in Idaho Inlet on Chicago Island.

The evening of the first night at anchor, crewmember Bruce Nelson and I were in the wheelhouse when we spotted deer coming down to the beach. We looked at each other and grinned. In Seattle I had bought a new compound bow and Bruce had a shotgun and a handful of slugs with him. Although we didn't have a skiff, we began to plan our hunt and came up with a way to get to the beach.

We decided to don survival suits, wrap our bow and shotgun in plastic, and swim to shore while towing a line to attach to the beach. This worked fairly well and we spent the next two days deer hunting while waiting out the weather. Bruce took one nice buck while I missed a couple and failed to get a deer. The weather cleared and we were on our way. We ate well the remainder of the trip, completely devouring Bruce's deer by the time we hit Kodiak.

At the start of the January 1989 season, we learned the pollock quota was going to a new fleet which was starting to boom—the American factory trawler fleet. This was the start of the heyday of factory trawlers and the Americanization of the fishing industry in Alaskan waters. American factory trawlers received preference over the JV catcher boats for the quotas because they could harvest the pollock quota and process it onboard while we would be delivering a raw product to be processed on a foreign vessel. We were forced to switch to other species.

We opted to fish again with Profish, the Korean market, and cod was the target. I decided three months of vacation wasn't enough and took the first part of 1989 off to ski at Alyeska Resort in Girdwood. By the time I met up with the *Dawn* in Dutch Harbor on March 1, the venture was switching to yellowfin sole fishing.

For some reason that now escapes me, the venture was shut down three weeks after we arrived until early fall. It was the middle of March and we found ourselves back in Kodiak with no real shoreside market and I was kicking myself for taking so much time off. By the time I paid my taxes for 1988, I was flat broke and desperate to make some money.

By late March we lined up a market to deliver bags to a rig called the *Alaskan Harvester*. We were going to fish Pacific ocean perch (POP) outside of Prince William Sound, which sounded great to me. We arrived in Seward on March 25 and learned our mothership was broken down. We proceeded to the fishing grounds in search of a body of POP while waiting for our mothership. As we anchored off of Hinchinbrook Island outside of Prince William Sound, we listened as the marine radio went wild. The Exxon Valdez had hit a reef just outside of Valdez and in the end spilled over 260,000 barrels of crude oil, with some later estimates as high as 750,000 barrels. Prince William Sound to the south Kodiak Archipelago and Alaska Peninsula would never be the same again for many years.

DEATH AND DESTRUCTION

The Exxon Oil Spill

Like a drunken fisherman leaving a bar, the Exxon Valdez departed Valdez Narrows just after midnight on March 24, 1989. Loaded with over a million barrels of North Slope crude oil, it plowed into Bligh Reef in Prince William Sound. "Oh shit" was heard around the world and madness resulted.

During the following days the marine radio came alive, with everyone wondering what was going on. Peggy Dyson, who had been giving weather forecasts to mariners in Alaskan waters twice a day at 8 a.m. and 6 p.m. since the 1970s, began asking for weather reports from the area. We were anchored within twenty-five miles of the spill and gave them to her two or three times a day.

I called and gave the Coast Guard the specs on the *Dawn* and told them we'd love to help if we could. Meanwhile, I was after the owner, Oral Burch, to get something lined up from his end in Kodiak. I vividly remember my crewmember, Bruce Nelson, asking me—joking I think—to radio the response team to ask if we could help. He was thinking there would be all kinds of women scientists, secretaries, and biologists we could offer many kinds of services to.

The first days after the spill were total mayhem and no one seemed to know what to do. If Exxon and the Coast Guard had acted right away, so much destruction could have been avoided. As it was, nothing was done during those first crucial days. We went for a look and were told to stay away. We were a 90-foot dragger with a ton of deck space, lots of horsepower, and a good strong crew right on the scene and begging to help. A vessel in the *Dawn's* size class could have carried enough containment booms to completely seal off the tanker and Bligh Reef. Instead, we were told by the Coast Guard to leave.

After being turned down, we departed April 1 for Kodiak. Our mothership was still broken down and Prince William Sound was now a national disaster area. It wasn't until April 10 that we were finally hired by Exxon to fight the spill. It took those idiots thirteen days to finally ask for assistance. I guess they needed to consult their lawyers, rather than common sense.

Kodiak was about 300 sea miles from Prince William Sound. The sludge from the spill was already working its way out of the sound and into the Gulf of Alaska. No one knew how far it would reach or the effects it would have. People were scared, worried, and quite angry. The oil spill was all anyone talked about. Salmon and herring seasons were just around the corner, and these fishermen were very concerned.

Just prior to getting the contract with Exxon we had rigged the *Dawn* for shore-based fishing. Now we had to strip the boat of all gear, nets, doors, sweeps, and codends. Everything came off. This was a very hectic time for Exxon, the Coast Guard, and Veco, the company placed in charge of the oil cleanup. The oil slick had moved westward with the tides and currents and had reached the southern coastline off the Kenai Peninsula. No one had any idea what to do about it and the opportunity to contain it within Prince William Sound had long since passed.

We were one of the six original boats hired in the cleanup effort that included trawlers from 60 to 90 feet long that were paired into three groups. Our partner boat, the *Hickory Wind*, was also based out of Kodiak and its skipper was Dennis Cox, Jr. The second pair consisted of the *Topaz* and *Sea Mac*, and the third pair was the *Tusing* and *Advantage*.

A television crew interviewed my crew and me the day we were rigging up and we ended up being on national TV. It was a good thing they didn't broadcast the whole tape. The TV crew was a last minute thing Grandpa had volunteered us for. We had been working all day offloading trawl gear and sucking down beer since 7 a.m. By mid-afternoon we were all somewhat drunk. I, the fearless captain, was hammered. We had also smoked a Bob Marley joint just thirty minutes before the TV crew showed up unexpectedly. An interview? Sure *mon*, I mean miss.

As the crew set up and started filming, Bruce Nelson came running by headed for the engine room. A film guy asked what he was doing.

"We're busy sinking," answered Ron Naughton, a huge Native American crewmember with a crooked smile.

We had been melting 20 tons of ice out of our fish hold, since that space would be needed for additional storage in our oil spill response. Someone had left a valve open on the bilge manifold without engaging the bilge pump. This meant water from the melting ice along with the seawater being pumped in to melt it was all going in the bilges without being pumped out. Luckily, Bruce was able to fix it within minutes. Meanwhile, I did the interview with my sunglasses on. My guys and I all had stupid grins plastered across our faces, trying not to look like a bunch of drunken fishermen, which we were.

By April 11, all six vessels were on our way to fight the spill. When we arrived at Nuka Bay, located west of Seward on the Kenai Peninsula, the oil had already dispersed into the Gulf of Alaska. All I could think about was what the hell took these guys so long to do something?

Someone higher up thought maybe they could get boats to break it up, since the slick was actually a mass. We ended up naming it mousse because it looked like a chocolate mousse dessert floating at sea. In actuality, it was heavily layered crude oil about a foot thick. When we first came across it, there were patches that would stretch for several square miles, moving with the wind, tides, and currents.

Initially we towed old shrimp and groundfish nets and old salmon seines on the surface of the water between two boats, trying to break up the mass in an effort to sink it. Out of sight, out of mind, put the stuff on the bottom of the ocean, seemed to be the thinking at the time by those in charge.

We began towing in Nuka Bay on April 12. Working with the *Hickory Wind*, we hooked bridles together and set about 20 fathoms of wire to tow the first old shrimp net. The floating oil sludge was about six inches thick and formed patties about the size of dinner plates. As we towed through a large area, the mousse would break up but not sink. Large clumps would break into smaller ones and a great sheen was formed upon the water. Instead of one big field of crude oil, we created many smaller pockets. I don't know if this method made it worse or actually helped matters. We definitely broke up the largest concentrations of the spill, but we also created a much larger area of floating death.

"I can't believe what they have done to Alaska," I wrote in my logbook.

We continued our work in front on Nuka Bay on April 13, starting at 7:30 a.m. The oil spots looked smaller but very thick and our busting up efforts looked in good shape. By 5:30 p.m. the winds had died, the sun came out, and much of the thick stuff had dispersed into a heavy sheen.

"Dead birds everywhere! Nothing alive showing," I noted in my logbook.

By April 14, the oil had turned the beaches black in the bay where we were working and our main consideration became the west side of the bay near Nuka Point. All six boats assisted in the effort to pound up the oil and we were able to break up a major concentration of the oil inside Nuka Bay. By the next day, however, the oil had moved even further into the bay on the east side. Reports of oil hitting Kodiak, Chiniak, and Shelikof Straight also began coming in.

We didn't find another body of oil until noon outside of Nuka Passage on April 16, and it was about the size of a football field. By 8:30 p.m. we had finished our day's work and anchored in Surprise Bay on the west arm of Nuka Bay. The Coast Guard held a meeting that evening on the cutter *Morganthaw* right next to us, but excluded all six fishing vessels and crews from participating. I called them on the radio and asked to be included, but was rejected. We all felt that our efforts were nothing but a sideshow and no one seemed interested in our ideas and thoughts.

Dennis and I finally received 500 meters of Norwegian containment booms at Port Dick, west of Nuka Bay, on April 17. The boom was made of very strong rubber and each individual section was about four feet long and consisted of a round floating top half about 24 inches in diameter. Attached to the bottom was a skirt, which was weighted and hung down into the water to a depth of around three feet.

The oil sludge was outside of Surprise Bay at this point. With a boat on each end, we planned to slowly tow the boom and form it into a half circle behind the two boats. One boat would take the boom out towards a concentration of oil mousse and the other boat would pick up the loose end, come abreast about one hundred yards off the first boat, and act like a unit to collect the body of oil inside the boom. This all looked good on paper.

On the first day we were able to fill the 500-meter boom with oil within forty-five minutes and then slowly towed it into an arm in Port Dick. We anchored in 10 fathoms of water and called the *Morganthaw*. We told them we had about 500 barrels of oil collected, the location, and asked for a skimmer to collect it. Dennis and I were feeling really proud of our day's work. We had successfully collected what we both estimated to be about 2,500–3,000 gallons of sludge and had managed to tow the boom inside a bay where there was no wind or swell. A skimmer would have had a very easy time collecting it from our boom.

The Coast Guard proceeded to tell us that there wasn't a skimmer available at the time and told us to monitor our boom until a skimmer could be freed to come to us. There were two skimmers on the overall scene and they were within five miles of our position. At the time, however, they were unsuccessfully trying to skim oil in open water outside of the bay unassisted.

The following day a skimmer still did not come to collect our oil. Again we called the Coast Guard and were told to wait and maintain the boom. By that afternoon, the wind had shifted into our bay and after a three hour battle with the boom, the oil washed up on a nice little beach and very quickly engulfed it.

I was angry beyond belief and let the higher ups know it. We probably would have been better off leaving the oil offshore than having it end up on that secluded beach. We later found out during those two days the two skimmers had only collected about one hundred gallons of oil because the swells were too big offshore. If they would have assisted us when we requested it, they could have collected thirty times that amount, plus it would have freed us up to collect more for them during that period.

To me this was just another example of how screwed up the Coast Guard and Exxon were in handling the cleanup. As stories were passed around, we learned the other four boats also had their share of suffering from the spill management team's horrible incompetence.

By April 18, quite a few more boats began to arrive four miles outside Port Dick. The weather had come up and was too severe to work the boom, so we headed back into the bay to try and work an area of the spill in more protected waters. We picked up a second section of the boom and towed 1,000 meters into the west arm of the bay. We then hooked up two booms and towed across the whole bay. The skimmer never showed up to take the oil, and our five hours of effort were once again wasted.

Sadly, my most vivid recollection about those first days of the cleanup is that nothing was alive in the area. There was no sign of fish in the water column or on the bottom expander, which is a feature on our echo sounder used for fishing that shows a video picture of the ocean floor. Seals, sea otters, and seabirds had also disappeared. From the point where we found the oil to ten miles out, nothing alive was visible on the water surface or on our sounder.

They have killed Alaska, I thought to myself.

When we first went to work for Exxon we had no idea how long we'd be gone. Food was now becoming a problem for all six boats. The Coasties flew in a couple of days' worth of supplies by helicopter, but more was needed. Our boat was elected to make a supply run and since Kodiak was close, we went there. We also wanted to pick up some more gear.

Bruce Nelson and I went shopping for the boats. The *Topaz* had an owner/operator who was a vegetarian and had given us a huge grocery list. I threw it out and blamed it on Bruce, all the while assuring Bruce, "No sweat, I'll remember it all." They wanted milk so I threw a case of coconut milk into the cart. For cheese, in went goat cheese. Bruce picked some bizarre unknown fruits from Asia that looked good enough for at least a reaction. For veggies we used the same method. Anything that looked like some kind of vegetable was fair game.

"They want it right?" we'd say, while tossing seven of them in the cart. The idea gained momentum and we were buying all sorts of produce that we had no idea what it was, let alone how to eat it. We must have looked like two mad men.

"What's this thing?" Bruce would ask with a smile.

"I don't know, but we better buy a couple of them. They might need it."

When we arrived back at the cleanup grounds, we transferred the food to the *Topaz*. They never said a word, but Bruce and I laughed so hard after it was delivered. We would have loved to have seen their faces when those starving guys opened up those boxes of food. We were never asked to buy groceries again but this single incident lightened up a very troublesome time for us and gave us something to laugh about, as sick as that may be.

For the next two weeks we chased the major body of oil up the coast towards the tip of the Kenai Peninsula and Cook Inlet. The tides and winds in this area around the Barren Islands are very severe, as the Gulf of Alaska, Shelikof Strait, and Cook Inlet all meet here and form some of the roughest waters anywhere in the world. Large concentrations of oil were broken up and oil was now turning up in many areas at the same time. Afognak Island, Upper Cook Inlet, the Alaska Peninsula, and Kodiak Island were all being hit.

We were assigned the mainland side of Shelikof Strait on the Alaska Peninsula. During the first five days of May we set up booms in the mouths of salmon streams, did beach surveys, reported contaminated beaches, and towed containment booms in open water concentrations. By this time we were only finding smaller isolated patches of floating mousse, which ranged in size from one to fifty barrels (fifty-five gallon drums). We regularly used barrels as units to estimate the size of a body of oil. For example, we would say, "We found a patch of mousse at 57°10' north, 156°20' west, with about twenty barrels worth."

There were still very few skimmers and the fleet of cleanup vessels had spread out over hundreds of miles of coastline. More times than not, we were on our own. After we collected sludge in our boom, we'd send the skiff to the boom to collect the mousse in five gallon buckets and bag it into heavy plastic bags—an extremely messy job. We'd then store the bags onboard until they could be dropped off on support vessels.

On May 6 we were called to Uyak Bay on the western side of Kodiak Island, which was getting hit hard. The area we were assigned was fairly protected, with booms set up in front of all the salmon streams. By this time there was not any mousse left in the open water.

Uyak Bay is a large bay with many arms leading into the island community of Larson Bay. Many salmon streams, hunting and fishing lodges, set net fishing sites, and lots of wildlife are in the area. Dennis on the *Hickory Wind* had a family set net fishing site located on Chief's Point at the northern end of the bay. We headed there first.

His cabin was tucked in a small, protected bay. We boomed off the entrance in an effort to keep the clam beaches safe. The type of boom we were deploying near streams and beaches was semi-absorbent material with six-inch floating tubes made up of a packed, shredded paper-type material. It was light, easy to deploy, and did a very good job of soaking up oil. I believe this one single method did by far the most good of all the cleanup work we were involved in. By this time, most of the oil was in the form of heavy sheens and the absorbent booms worked best. I'd like to think that we saved beaches and streams that otherwise would have been destroyed.

On May 10 we received a Swedish boom made up of square sections. Its flexibility allowed us to wind the complete boom up on our net reel, making it convenient to store, set out, and collect back. For the first time we were able work as a single boat operation by towing it off our outrigger. A Navy skimmer was finally in the area and at last we had an easy way to release the oil we had accumulated inside the booms. The cleanup effort began working as a unit and was busy, as effective methods were used.

I rotated off the boat at the end of May and headed for the Kenai River for one of the best salmon and trout seasons ever. In June and July of 1989 there wasn't any commercial fishing for salmon due to the spill and the Kenai River was alive with salmon. In later years we found out that over-escapement was as bad as not enough fish getting to spawning streams, but that summer of sport fishing will live in my memory forever.

In mid-July I rotated back onboard to continue with the cleanup effort. The *Dawn* was still in Uyak Bay and assigned to a group of beaches. We would visit each beach site daily and collect contaminated oil bags gathered by workers on the shore. We'd then deliver the bags to a barge. We were glorified garbage collectors. With the long days of summer in Alaska, we'd start our route around 4 p.m. and finish up at the barge around 9 or 10 p.m. This left the mornings and early afternoons free to sport fish, and did we ever take advantage of this.

By early August we were working along Zachar Bay off of Kodiak Island. Bruce and I were fly fishing for dog salmon during a break and Terry, a third crewman, was a couple hundred yards upstream. Bruce and Terry had seen a huge bear there the day before, so Bruce and I decided it was a prime opportunity to play a practical joke on Terry. We took out our 44 magnum pistols used for bear protection and each fired a couple of rounds into the air before running downstream towards the skiff screaming, "Bear! Bear!"

Terry went up the first tree he came to. We left him there for about three hours before he realized he'd been had. He didn't talk to us for days, and this is how we ended our Exxon contract. We constantly messed with Terry and had the time of our lives doing so.

By August 10, our role in the cleanup effort was over and we went through a very thorough boat cleaning as we rigged the *Dawn* for fall Bering Sea JV fishing. I'd like to believe that we did do some good working for Exxon those 4-1/2 months. They paid our vessel $4,400 a day plus all expenses, amounting to over a half million dollars for our effort.

To this day I believe Exxon's main goal in the cleanup and response effort was public relations. They spent large sums of money buying off people and boats. The cleanup effort was massive, but too little was done in the early stages of the spill. And like so many others, we took advantage of the situation. I know of people who made a lot of money off of Exxon's open wallet. Even though I had some great times that summer, the black beaches and dead birds, otters, and even whales, haunt my memory.

The greatest shame regarding the cleanup effort is that the oil spill was in Prince William Sound, which is a bay. It's an awfully big area, but it's still a bay. There are a number of islands on the outer edge of the sound, with the largest being about seven miles wide. If Exxon and the Coast Guard had acted right away, they could have flown in enough containment booms to seal off the Sound and prevent the oil from escaping into the Gulf of Alaska.

To this day I have a bad taste in my mouth for the way management handled the spill, especially the initial response team. They sat on their bureaucratic butts wondering what they should do while their mess destroyed entire ecosystems.

The effects from the spill live on today. My response to the statement that there's no long-term effect from the spill and that the cleanup was successful is to ask the Sound herring fishermen why their herring had open lacerations for years or ask shrimp fishermen how well they're doing nowadays. The over-escapement that occurred to many salmon streams continues to have a domino effect on salmon life cycles. Even twelve years after that fateful night in 1989, if you walked certain beaches you could still find layers of oil by digging down four inches into the rocks and sand in areas that Veco pronounced clean.

In addition to severely impacting Alaska's fisheries in South Central Alaska, the Exxon Valdez oil spill caused injury and death at every trophic level of life in the sea. It is estimated between 100,000 and 300,000 seabirds were killed, with the common murre colonies likely reduced by half. Approximately 2,650 sea otters were killed, with possible long-term effects on their population.

Yes, I'm still bitter and feel it's a crime that Exxon was able to successfully sue their insurance company and tie up relief funds to fishermen and communities for long years. Although Exxon was at the core of the problem, the Coast Guard and Veco should also share the blame for their incompetence, poor planning, and terrible management. My initial hope was that everyone learned from the mistakes made and a disaster of this magnitude would never be allowed to occur again. Yet when the Deepwater Horizon drilling rig exploded on April 20, 2010, gushing oil into the Gulf of Mexico for months and decimating marine life, the madness that resulted during the response effort was all too familiar and sad.

FALL VENTURE 1989

The Joint Venture Era Comes To An End

It was now back to JV fishing. I was again signed up with the Russian venture MRC and again the Russians didn't have enough motherships. We were included in a pool effort, which was thought to be the best way for boats to deal with a limited market. The Russians had five motherships on the grounds and twenty-four catcher boats. This broke down to around $3,000 per catcher a day for 25 tons (one tow) of fish. The promise of more motherships was always there but never materialized. I quickly rebelled.

On the very first day I began to develop outside markets and made those my priority. Soon I was once again the fleet's black sheep. The *Topaz* had a young new skipper, Lando, who became angry at me for these outside tows. Years later, I still imagine him fuming about it. I'd be making three to four tows a day while he was drifting twenty or more hours.

This time around it took the Russians twenty-four days to kick me out. Or was it I quit because it took twenty-four days to find a full-time market? All I clearly remember is that they were mad again and I was extremely glad. The new market I found was with my old friends on the Japanese ship, *Oke Bono No. 1*. The American JV rep from the previous year, Stu, was back and we finished off the yellowfin sole season in late November with a half million dollar boat gross.

With my income in six digits and my taxes paid, 1989 turned out to be a very good year. That winter I went to Girdwood, skied three months, and bought a beautiful house with a great view of Mt. Alyeska. Girdwood became my permanent home.

The JV era officially ended in 1990. With the help of our foreign friends, the Americans had learned to fish a new fishery. It was a good situation for both sides, since it allowed the foreigners to continue to catch fish as they worked alongside us. We basically acquired their knowledge of the groundfish fishery that had been previously unknown to us, and then said, "Thank you very much, goodbye."

The catcher boats delivering to the foreigners had almost all American captains and crews, with only a handful of Norwegians and other Europeans thrown in. The foreign boats seemed a different part of the operation even though they were the same size boats as the rest of us. Nonetheless, we had all been in it together. At times while fishing in the Bering Sea in an 86-foot southern style bender with 40-foot waves and 60-knot winds, the world can be an ugly place.

Since the time had come that the Americans were ready to branch out on our own, our government began the domestic fishery program, where only vessels with 51 percent U.S. ownership or more were allowed to fish Alaska's waters. That's not to say the foreigners didn't find ways to work around this roadblock, especially when they could find a national with dual citizenship who was more than happy to reap the figurehead profits.

A realistic look at the worldwide fishing structure makes the true bottom line clear. It's all about business. Like anywhere, where there is money to be made, someone's boat will always be ready in the commercial fishing world. We, as American fishermen, have traditionally been one step behind the pack, while Japan, Norway, and Denmark have track records at being the leaders.

The Bering Sea was the hot spot in the world at this time. The 51 percent ownership requirement was nothing more than an inconvenience to most foreigners. The right partners were found. In one case, the ex-wife of a Japanese businessman became the 51 percent owner of a factory trawler fleet that continues to fish Alaska's waters today. It was common knowledge among management crew on her vessels that her first language was Japanese, her first home was in Japan, but she had a U.S passport and a second home in the U.S. How convenient. Her ex-husband, in the meantime, owned vessels called trampers that bought the fish "her" fleet caught and transported them to Japan.

To make matters worse, it was rumored the company only claimed about a quarter of the actual price paid for the fish sold to the ex-husband's tramper. In other words, they allegedly only paid U.S. taxes on about a quarter of the product sold. What an operation. And we allowed it. NMFS at one time started an investigation that they later claimed couldn't be validated. So they focused on American fishermen instead.

The Japanese continued to spend millions buying into and revamping shoreside plants. Surimi processing plants to make imitation crabmeat out of pollock sprung up what seemed like overnight in Dutch Harbor and Kodiak. Today these plants also own a large percentage of the catcher boats who supply their product, some of which were once JV boats. These boats are unrecognizable today from their early years, due to numerous widening and lengthening metamorphoses they have gone through in West Coast shipyards. Today most Alaskan shoreside plants and many of the factory trawlers are owned by the Japanese, one way or another.

During this time the Norwegians and other European countries went the other way. Their banks financed huge sums of money to build new state of the art factory trawlers, from head and gut boats to huge

350-foot surimi trawlers. The head and gut boats were usually 100 feet and up in length, and got their name from removing the heads and guts from fish before freezing the whole fish body until it was sold for reprocessing on shore (usually in Asian countries). Surimi boats are strictly midwater pollock and hake boats that are capable of running close to a million pounds of fish a day through their factories. They mince the fish product into a paste that is bleached, flavored, and dyed to make it look and taste like crab. Personally, I avoid eating the stuff.

I figure the Norwegian involvement goes back to the daring days of the hard-traveling Vikings. Now they like to go to other countries and catch their fish, since their own fishing is limited. At least they don't kill you now.

Today money still tracks back to foreign countries far too often. The two big players in Alaska continue to be the Norwegians and the Japanese, although I think they're in it for different reasons. The Japanese stay in to keep the supply coming their way, the price reasonable, and to maintain the best quality as possible, for a country that fish is a much-desired staple. The Norwegians are for making money catching other peoples' fish. The Danish seem to also act the same way, and I think way back when the Vikings knocked up all the Danish women on their way through, they transported their genes.

Many factory trawlers take along a Japanese quality control technician at great expense (upwards of $10,000 a month) to protect against Japanese claims that the product they've purchased is damaged or inferior. The Japanese used to buy 90–100 percent of the fish caught in the late 1980s, all the way through to the mid-1990s. As a domestic market developed for the fish in America, current markets now only sell around half of the fish to Asian countries. Even so, it's still enough to warrant a foreign technician.

The technicians work shifts in the factory (usually eight hours on, eight hours off), working alongside the factory foreman to ensure quality control. They check pan weights and sizing to be sure it's accurate, make sure the fish is taken out of the freezer at the proper core temperature, and do some fish handling. Most of them work as an overseer of the factory operation.

A good technician is like having another foreman onboard. They train the processors and help move the best personnel to the best positions. Good technicians stay with boats for years. I had one Japanese technician, Sugi, stay with me for five years on two different boats. He basically followed me (along with his company) until he retired. If a technician likes a particular captain or crew, they insist on going back to them. In essence, they become part of the family onboard.

Sugi showed me a picture of his daughter who was a few years younger than me the first time I met him. From that day forward, I teased him I was going to go to Japan and marry his daughter, which— to say lightly—he didn't care for. But it was a surefire way to get him out of the wheelhouse and back in the factory.

Shore-based fish plants nearly all have Japanese money behind them. And for factory trawlers, they are known to throw a half million dollar loan your way to help with the cost of installing a new factory. Of course, you have to sell them most of your fish.

While I've really trashed the Russian ventures, I now look back and truly appreciate taking part in that fishery. What we did in those days will live forever in my soul. I delivered fish to Chinese, Polish, Russian, Korean, and Japanese vessels, and met people from many different cultures. In seeing firsthand how they lived and worked, I learned that fishermen are the same no matter what country they are from. We all go to sea for the same reasons.

The communist Russia I saw was a lot different than our diplomats saw at that time. During the cold war that lasted through the 1980s, our countries were in essence enemies, and didn't trust one another. There was an element of fear involved. We as fishermen, however, could sit at the same table, drink vodka, talk about women and fishing, and we were friends, even comrades. Just a bunch of fishermen. Really all the same.

I took those years for granted back then. I was very young, hotheaded, and foolish. I wish that I could have that opportunity again, knowing what I know today.

* * *

Until this time, most of the fishing in Alaska was being done by catcher boats that were equipped to catch and hold the fish only, before delivering their catch to shoreside processing plants or to foreign factory ships at sea that were able to do the processing. While some fishing was still allowed by foreign fishing vessels in U.S. waters, the Magnuson-Stevens Fisheries and Conservation Management Act was phasing it out. A 200-mile limit was imposed on foreigners fishing in U.S. waters. If foreigners wanted fish, they had to buy them from American boats and fishermen, or work with them in a JV fishing program.

Factory trawlers were the first to follow the JV fishery. There was one total allowable catch (TAC) for all the boats each season, with a maximum amount of tonnage for each species. The American catcher boats and factory trawlers had first dibs on the TAC. American boats began delivering their catch to motherships owned and crewed by foreign countries. The major players were Russia, Japan, China, Poland, and South Korea, although a few other countries would send a boat or two now and then. If the American boats couldn't catch the TAC, the foreign boats would then have the right to fish directly.

The JV years were relatively few. During this time I delivered codends to a handful of really smart American fishermen and the foreigners. Those years became a bridge to foreign power and influence that continues today on Alaskan waters. The Japanese bought up a handful of tuna seiners that were converted to factory trawlers, which later became the Fishing Company of Alaska. They also invested millions into shore plants all over the coastal villages of Alaska. I wish I could have seen the big picture back then, but who did?

The Scandinavians, who had been kicked off the East Coast, also began pouring money into the new factory trawler fleet being built, with Norway and Denmark leading the way. Boats fishing Alaskan waters had to be American built, so they worked their way around the law by sending an American-built 80-foot trawler to Norway or Korea for refurbishing. There they would cut the keel out, throw away the old shell, and convert it to a 300-foot modern factory trawler.

To this day I am angered by what was allowed to happen. There is no way Norway would let the Americans go to Norway, buy a small boat, bring it back to America and turn it into a huge fishing machine that would then return to fish Norwegian waters with an American fishmaster at the helm, much less let us then ship all the product out of the country. It would never happen even back in 1930, much less today. They simply would not allow the bullshit that we continue to allow in our waters.

This is where the term paper skipper came to be known in Alaskan fisheries. To this day, foreigners continue to have huge financial interests in fishing our waters. They bring onboard their own fishmasters to direct the fishing onboard, and hire an American captain and crew to meet the percentage required by law. Far too often, the American captain spends his days in the wheelhouse (where his presence is required by law) drinking coffee, smoking cigarettes, pleasure reading, and oh yeah, taking care of paperwork while the ever-present fishmaster monitors the fishfinders and controls the operation.

SHORE-BASED FISHING

We entered the 1990s very down. JV fishing was a thing of the past. Oral Burch, who had become like a father to me, was diagnosed with colon cancer and was given six to ten months to live. Everyone was shocked.

Although shore-based fishing wasn't new to me, I had always seen it as more of a filler to pass the time in between JV seasons. I had delivered to various plants in Kodiak on and off for the past four years, but never took it seriously.

The factory trawler fleet was now in its heyday and they could harvest all the fish quotas available. The smaller JV trawlers and new larger refrigerated sea water (RSW) boats were developing a strong shore-based fishery, bringing in pollock and cod to shoreside plants. The RSW rigs could pack upwards of a million pounds of fish and it seemed like all the JV boats were being lengthened and widened to compete.

New plants to handle these boats were popping up all over the coasts, from Kodiak to the Pribilof Islands. Remote places like Akutan, Cold Bay, and King Cove were now big players in the groundfish boom. The fishery was in a midst of great changes and huge fleet development. If you didn't change along with it, you were quickly left behind.

From my standpoint and also to a great extent the Burch brothers, we were in a state of shock. I didn't want to believe the JV days were over. When you're in your twenties and making six figures a year, you never believe it will end. I spent my money as fast as I made it. I made terrible investments and just flat believed that that kind of money would always be easy to obtain. Boy did reality suck.

For the March 1990 pollock season our market was with Alaska Pacific Seafoods in Kodiak. They had a new surimi plant that produced imitation crabmeat and the plant was hungry for fish. To supply enough fish they hired some big guns from Seattle, the large RSW rigs. Known as the three A boats, these 120-foot rigs packed around a half million pounds of fish and it seemed like there was always one at the dock offloading fish.

On the *Dawn* we only packed 170,000 pounds of fish, so we were always getting bumped in favor of one these A boats. The fish were only worth 6¢ a pound and we had to wait at the dock to get offloaded, making our weekly gross very little. I began to quickly develop a bad taste for the business.

We switched over to fishing for cod by late March since they were worth 15¢ a pound, more than twice that of pollock. We did a little better but still weren't making anywhere near the money we were used to. I was after the Burch brothers to lengthen and widen the *Dawn* and to install a RSW tank, since at the time we were still icing our fish. Almost the entire JV fleet was absorbed into the new shoreside fishery and most boats were quick to make huge changes to their boats to enable them to pack more tonnage. Small 80-foot boats would come out of the shipyard 120 feet long and 35 feet wide. The Burch brothers didn't want to spend that kind of money and the relationship between us started to suffer.

When it was my turn to rotate off in May, I had only made about $8,000. I jumped over to Richard McLellan's boat, the *Irene's Way*, to give him a break and try to make a little more money.

If the *Dawn's* market was bad, his was a nightmare. Richard delivered to a Greek who was so dishonest that hardly anyone would sell him fish. The guy was later run out of Kodiak. Still, it was the only market Richard had and while I was running his boat I slowly worked my way in with the All Alaskan Seafoods plant, a very good market at the time.

We fished for Dover sole, which included a bycatch of black cod. The Dovers are deep-water flatfish which sold for 5¢ a pound. The black cod was the money fish and was worth $1–1.50 a pound, depending on their size. We were allowed 20 percent round weight on Dover sole, so if we had 100,000 pounds of Dovers (worth $5,000) we could have 20,000 pounds of black cod (worth $20,000). This was good money, particularly if we could do a couple of trips a week.

We were filling the boat in a couple of days on this venture, but what we were getting paid versus what went over the dock were two very different things. On one trip I filled Richard's boat with Dovers and what I estimated to be 20 percent black cod and a few red rockfish. The total estimate was around 150,000 pounds of marketable fish. I split the delivery between the Greek and All Alaskan, with the majority of black cod and red rockfish going to All Alaskan. When I received the fish tickets from both plants, I ended up with a total of 80,000 pounds of Dovers, 11,000 pounds of black cod, and 5,000 pounds of rockfish. The other 50,000 pounds of Dovers and who knows how much black cod and rockfish were listed as discards by the Greek and I didn't get paid for it.

The plants were high-grading like mad and picking only the best fish for processing. Meanwhile, I was paid next to nothing. It was a crime and as time continued I started to hate this new fishery.

Corky Decker, 13, holding a fish caught on the *Marion* (1975).

Marion returning to Perkins Cover after a day of fishing (Ogunquit, Maine).

DEEP SEA FISHING
Aboard The
MARION

46 FOOT HEAD BOAT
WITH SUN CANOPY

We Go Way Out - Sonar Fish Finder - Bait Furnished and Rod & Reels
Privacy for Ladies - Flush Toilets - Radio Telephone -   Radar
- Up to Date Life Saving and Fire Fighting Equipment - US Coast Guard Approved
42 Passengers - Reliable Licensed Ocean Operator

Leaves Perkins Cove, Ogunquit, Maine, Between 8^{30} and 9 a. m.
Returns 2^{30} - 3 p. m. -   MAY 30 to OCTOBER 30
FOR RESERVATIONS
CALL WELLS   646-3284

Captain Voorhis

Brochure used to advertise fishing aboard the *Marion* (Ogunquit, Maine).

Let's go fishing aboard the No. 1 Deep Sea Fishing Boat
in Perkins Cove. We've been here for 15 years. The
MARION is the only true party fishing vessel. It's not
a converted "dragger" or "lobster boat" as it was built
only for fishing comfort and safety. Plenty of open
deck to move around on, canopy and cabin to keep you out
of sun and rain. 42" rail so your kids won't fall overboard. You ride in this boat, not on it and you don't
need a six foot gaff and stand on your head to get a fish.
The MARION is 46 feet in length, 14 feet wide with draft
of 3 1/2 feet and is powered by a big Detroit Diesel engine that moves it along at 14 knots.
The MARION is manned by a crew of three. Your captain,
an ex-serviceman with over 15 years of sea and party
fishing experience. A first mate, also an ex-serviceman
with plenty of sea service and deck hand who can filet
or gaff a fish quicker than you can blink your eye.
The MARION is a U.S. documented Coast Guard inspected 42
passenger vessel with up-to-date lifesaving and firefighting equipment. We have one of the finest fish finding machines on the market. Radio telephone, privacy for
ladies with flush toilets. So you owe it to yourself -
spend a day at sea and enjoy big boat comfort for you and
yours aboard the MARION, the finest deep sea fishing boat
in the Cove.

Narrative inside the *Marion* brochure.

Corky, 11, and Al Voorhis next to Al's car, advertising a day of fishing
aboard the *Marion* (1973).

Bleeding bluefin tuna (Maine).

The *Dawn* docked in Dutch Harbor (1990).

Oral Burch, co-owner of the *Dawn* and *Dusk* (Kodiak).

Burch Brothers
Box 2203
Kodiak, Alaska 99615
486 - 5238 or 486 - 3653

March 4, 1987

Mr. Jay Decker,

Hi, finally chased this darned form down, it is a copy of the one sent to Corky. He is one busy boy today trying to get out of Dutch Harbor by 3ᵖᵐ today. He sure is excited about the Dawn, In fact is madly in love with the boat. I told him he had a good boat under him, and don't think he believed me at first, now he is telling me how good our boat is.

You have a very good son in that boy. A beautiful worker and ambitious. He will make good in this country.

Hope you can read this writing.

Sincerely

Oral L. Burch

Letter from Oral Burch to Corky's father.

114

View of Dutch Harbor and Iliuliuk Bay from Bunker Hill.
Located on the island of Unalaska in the Aleutian Islands, Dutch Harbor is
800 air miles from Anchorage, Alaska.

Corky beside the factory trawler *Prosperity* (1995).

Barb Gimlin overlooking Kodiak harbor in 1994 during a break from her
fisheries observing duties.

Corky inspecting a load of fish onboard the *Prosperity* (1995).

This photo shows how quickly ice can build on the rails from sea spray.

When ice begins to build on deck, crews must keep on top of breaking it off (Rebecca Irene, March 1998).

Corky in the wheelhouse of the *Prosperity* (1995).

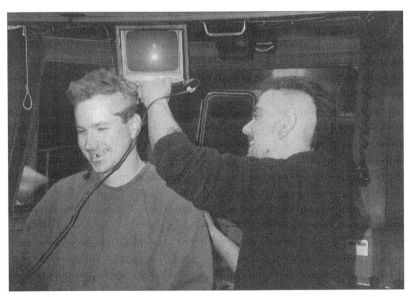

Mohawks were the call of the day in 1995 aboard the *Prosperity* when we were all sea-crazed. We all got them and even sent home a guy that was getting married in a week with one.

View of the net from the wheelhouse of the *Rebecca Irene* (1998).

Killer whales return every summer to Unimak Pass feeding grounds.
Above they enjoy a meal from the discard chute of the *Rebecca Irene.*

The *Rebecca Irene* and Corky's story *Sole on Ice* made the cover of *National Fisherman* for the May 2000 issue.

While many of the halibut caught as bycatch are the size of dinner plates, some monster halibut are occasionally caught that weigh over 400 pounds (*Gold Rush*, 1993).

Eagles are a common occurrence in Dutch Harbor and frequently visit boats, offering an up-close view.

Crab pots littering the sea floor pose a problem for trawlers when caught in their nets.

Bob Carter, a Maine Maritime Academy grad,
is the best engineer I have ever had.

Mending the net at sea.

For those of you have ever wondered how imitation crab is made, it starts with a minced paste of fish parts, being prepared in the photo above aboard the *Pacific Scout*.

Barb Gimlin at her NMFS fisheries observer station in the factory of the
Prosperity (October 1994).

This is the deck that Harold Tuttle and Corky built, with a view of
Mt. Alyeska in Girdwood, Alaska, in the background.

Not your typical childhood. Dancia, age 2, checks out a survival suit.

Corky, Barb, Dancia, and Jamie aboard the Jack of Hearts at Semiahmoo
Marina, Blaine, Washington (2000).

Sailing vessel *Jack of Hearts* underway in the San Juan Islands (2000).

Corky, Dancia, and Jamie catching dinner aboard the *Jack of Hearts* in
Hawaii (2002).

Barb, Dancia and Jamie relax aboard the *Jack of Hearts* while anchored off of Kauai (2002).

A HALIBUT DERBY

A halibut opening was coming up, so I convinced the owner of Richard's boat to gear up for this fishery. After all, how difficult could longlining for halibut be? Put out a bunch of baited hooks and haul 100-pound slabs of big fish onboard. Get paid. Nothing to it I thought. We had three weeks before the 24-hour opening. The boat had to be rigged from scratch and gear had to be built.

One of my two Irish deckhands had quite a bit of longlining experience. John was put in charge of designing the deck. He and Patty were both from Ireland, in their early twenties, and had been in the states for a couple of years.

We spent in excess of $30,000 on gear, haulers, tubs, and racks needed for longlining. We did almost all the work ourselves except for actually building the racks and table. This work was hired out to Paul Chevinak, a master craftsman who was able to make them out of wood and then fiberglass and gel coat them. We finished about three days before the opening.

I talked to my old crewmember Bruce Nelson, who had quit to pursue a career in art. He agreed to come along. The boat was rigged very well and had 15,000 hooks on 125 skates (tubs of gear). Along with Bruce, my two Irish guys, and a guy named Teddy from Poland, we baited the 15,000 hooks by hand with frozen octopus, squid, and cod.

When we departed Kodiak 36 hours before the opening we still had over 5,000 hooks to bait. So far we had spent $30,000 in rigging the boat, $4,000 in bait, $1,500 in fuel, and another $500 or so in food and miscellaneous expenses. Three weeks of working sixteen hours a day was all riding on one 24-hour opener and only Bruce and John had any real experience in longlining. It was a $36,000 gamble.

We decided that we'd set all of our gear the first part of the opening, then we'd have the remainder of the time to fill the boat with fish. This was mistake number one. Mistake number two was deciding to set all our gear in one area so we didn't waste time steaming around looking for the buoys that mark the gear. Not doing any research or talking with guys who spent time in this business was mistake number three.

The opening gun sounded at noon on a sunny May day off the south end of Kodiak, south of Chirikof Island. Boats were scattered everywhere and we found a nice open area with no one within four miles. The bottom sand had a nice gradual edge shallowing up into a rockier bottom closer to the island. It looked like a good spot to me. I had never towed in the area because it was inside a no trawl zone. Not having scouting data quickly became mistake number four.

We set all 15,000 hooks in five long strings of 3,000 hooks per set. We set one right after the other and our buoys were within a few boat lengths of each other. We set the strings towards the island, starting in 60 fathoms (360 feet) and ending in 30 fathoms (90 feet). The setting went fast and very smooth. All five strings were out in two hours and we had twenty-two hours remaining to get paid.

I steamed back towards the first buoy we set. The weather was flat calm and the guys were all eating, since we thought this would be our last chance to eat for quite some time. It took us under an hour to come alongside that first buoy. As I slowed down and kicked the boat out of gear, the *Irene* slowly came along with the flag end creeping down our starboard side. I slid her into reverse, gave the throttle some power, and—nothing. No reverse or anything.

135

Down I went to the engine room. I thought for sure the linkage had come off the reverse gear, but it was still attached. I returned to the wheelhouse and tried forward and reverse from the main station. Nothing happened. I freaked. Next I checked the oil in the gear, which was fine. The shaft was spinning in the engine room and the cables to the gear were fine. It had to be—oh no—the shaft. We had broken the main shaft that goes to the propeller.

We had 10 tons of ice piled in the shaft alley. All five of us moved that pile in two hours. The inspection hatches were removed and the problem was discovered. The tail shaft had come apart at the flange and slid all the way back. It was jammed against the stuffing box, which contains a type of bearing used for the rudder and propeller shafts.

Patty located all the bolts that had backed off in the shaft bilge and the five of us discussed the situation. We decided to try chainfalls to slide the tail shaft forward and back in place. We rigged up the falls, which each had a pulling power of five tons, and tried to slide the shaft to the flange. We needed to move it about sixteen inches, but it was jammed and wouldn't budge.

After shifting the falls and trying different angles with no success, I decided to force the issue with the hydraulics. We fareleaded the 25-ton pullmaster with our tow blocks into the fish hole, which entailed rigging the cable from the winch in order to get a straight pull. At the controls I gently eased the slack out of the cable and then applied 25 tons of ballard pull. The shaft pulled free and slammed up to the plate.

By now the stuffing box was leaking quite badly and we were busy trying to keep from sinking. I remember talking to another fisherman on the radio who asked how I was doing. "I'm busy sinking and can't talk right now," I said. The next thing I knew, a C-130 Coast Guard plane was buzzing us. It took some explaining to convince them we were cool and handling the situation.

Bruce managed to tighten up the stuffing box (while working in a couple feet of iced-down seawater) and stopped the leak. I pumped the hole dry and the flanges were bolted back together. It was 7 p.m., leaving us only seventeen hours to haul in our gear.

The first flag end came onboard and as the first hook came over the rail we discovered a costly error. Setting in a sand bottom meant sand fleas. Every fish that came onboard, including halibut, cod, and skate, was nothing but a shell of skin and bone with the flesh just gone. Over 300 pounds of halibut had been literally eaten up by these parasites. We were able to retrieve our gear quickly since there wasn't any quality halibut coming aboard to slow us down, but it didn't offer much comfort.

As we arrived at the shallower sets, the bottom hardened up and we started to see some live fish. The problem in the shallow water was the halibut were very small, with 95 percent under the legal limit of thirty-six inches.

When the last hook came aboard about 10 a.m. the following morning, we had less than 5,000 pounds of sellable halibut. The only plus of the whole trip was that we were able to retrieve all our gear. The halibut opening was a broker. The overhead and operating costs for bait, fuel, food, and ice were more than the fish sold for. We lost a lot of money in three weeks of very hard work and didn't make a dime.

SHORE-BASED CHANGES

In Kodiak the *Irene's Way* was cleaned up and Richard took it to Seward for shipyard work, while I went back on rotation on the *Dawn*. Grandpa Burch was fighting for his life as cancer slowly consumed him. In early June he still had his senses and spent almost all his time on his pleasure boat fishing for halibut and enjoying the summer.

Cod fishing that summer was incredible. Kodiak had a lot of new boats arriving in the area, most of which were JV boats from Oregon and Seattle. The new boats didn't know the waters and areas around the island yet, so our hot spots were safe, at least for a while.

Robbie, a crewman from the *Hickory Wind* and *Topaz,* was skippering a new boat brought in from the East Coast. He had been around Kodiak for a long time and I teamed up with him. The two of us were constantly on the fish, putting over a million pounds of fish a month in our fish holds during the hot months of July and August. By September the cod began to break up and it was quite a bit slower. The new boats on the scene began hitting the hot spots hard, so we switched over to deepwater flatfish to finish off the season.

By mid-September Grandpa was fading fast. He lost over 70 pounds and looked like a shell of who he was. On the first of October I said my goodbyes to him and went back to Girdwood knowing I wouldn't see him again. Oral Burch died October 16, 1990. I lost a good friend and the state of Alaska lost a pioneer. He was a great man. Even though I am not a religious person I do believe that he is looking over my shoulder or beside me in the wheelhouse every day I'm at sea.

Times were changing in more ways than one. To make it in this new shoreside fishery we had to modernize the boats. Early the following year I tried to convince Oral's brother Al of this. He wanted no part of spending any money on the two boats. Al got everything of Oral's down to the man's truck and tools. He was now the sole owner of the *Dawn* and *Dusk*, which were paid for free and clear from our hard work and his dead brother's management. Al is a politician, however, not a fisherman. I gave it six months, saw no future working with the remaining Burch brother, and decided to turn to factory trawlers, a fleet that was rapidly reaching its peak.

BACK TO SCHOOL

In order to operate one of the factory trawlers (also known as freezer trawlers, in the beginning) I needed to have a Coast Guard license. This, I learned, would be quite a task. Just to get into school I had to collect all my sea time, get letters of recommendation from three people, and take a drug test, physical, and eye exam—not to mention passing an armory of tests. I chose the Alaska Vocational Technical Center (AVTEC) in Seward for my sea school and radar portions, but had to go to New Orleans for firefighting school.

Firefighting came up first on the schedule. Houston Marine in New Orleans is associated with the best firefighting schools in the world for marine vessels, and their instructors are all heads of different fire department districts in New Orleans. That's where I decided to go.

The first two days were spent in the classroom with movies and lectures, ending with a written test. The following five days involved hands-on training at their training facility located ten miles from the hotel where most of the class stayed. The training area was isolated, fenced in, and looked like a secret military base.

We were led to a locker room and given old soot-covered foul weather gear and boots before meeting up at a bleacher-style bench to meet the instructors. Out of thirty students and four instructors, I happened to be the only Northerner and became known as the Yankee.

A huge X was placed on back of my rain jacket with duct tape. Great. I didn't like the way training was starting out.

For the next three days I became the class volunteer. "Okay, here we have an electrical fire. I need a volunteer to show everyone how to put it out. Where's that Yankee?"

Soon I forgot my own name. The guys were introducing me on Bourbon Street during our off hours as Yankee.

The last day of field testing was conducted in the hell hole, which held one person in a simulated bilge fire that had only one way in and no venting. The metal building used for it was twenty feet by twenty feet with a grated floor. Diesel fuel floating in a foot of water under the grating was ignited and the instructors waited until the walls were good and hot before opening the door. It was well named.

I was, of course, the volunteer to go first. I remember looking in that room thinking it couldn't be done. I was armed with only a fire hose and no breathing apparatus. Rosie, one of the instructors, yelled in my ear, "Don't worry Yankee, I'll yank you out before you're well done," and gave me a boot through the door.

Amazingly, the fire did go out and I remembered everything I was supposed to do. Then came the hard part. When the fire was out you were to stay in the hell hole, full of thick black smoke, for ten seconds while looking for flare-ups and breathing off the nozzle of the fire hose. I held my breath. The whole thing lasted about two minutes but seemed like thirty. I came out of the hole covered in soot, hacking, coughing and actually smiling.

The entire course was well run and used real fires that were extremely dangerous. I learned a great deal about fires in that one week and today I can say it was the best training I've ever had. Before I said my goodbyes to the instructors I gave each one a condom, Rosie a Kodiak hat, and told them to be careful on Bourbon Street.

People who fight fires are a different breed of men and women. Someone who actually goes into a burning structure has got to be the definition of what true bravery is. They put their lives at risk willingly and I have a great deal of respect for this profession. I had a firsthand look into their lives and am better for it. To me, these people are the real heroes of America.

The next leg of my education took place in Seward at AVTEC, with radar classes starting in early September. I figured radar would be a piece of cake since I had been using it my whole life. I knew everything about it. No problem.

An English chap named Dennis Lodge was the instructor. He had a special humorous wit about him that can only come naturally to a person. Dennis was born to be a teacher. During the next seven days I found out that I didn't know the first thing about radar.

Day one was on how radar works and what parts do what. It was all well and good, but who really cares except for maybe the Japanese and a few electronic wizards. I cared only that the damn thing came on when I hit the button.

The following three days we learned how to do radar plots in relative motion. This was really interesting and gave new insight on radar use. Today's radar has plotting features that convert relative motion to true motion and a north up display, which basically means the machine does the plotting for you.

At sea on the big boats we also use an automatic radar plotting aid (ARPA). These high-priced machines have on-screen readouts which include the closest point of approach for each target (such as a boat), time to the closest point of approach, bow crossing range, bow crossing time, and the bearing speed and course of the targets. To have this amazing technology at your fingertips all you need is a lot of money. A good ARPA sells for around $60,000, but is invaluable when a fleet of twenty or more boats is fishing within a six-mile area.

I became proficient at manual paper plots after doing around fifty in three days. Then we moved on to simulators with an actual radar hooked up to a central computer that Dennis programmed targets into. After a couple of simulator drills I became convinced that the English are a bit twisted. Dennis would program helicopters, hydrofoils, and anything else that did about 60 knots into that thing. I'd come out of the radar room shaking and he'd just smile and say, "Well lad, he come up on ya a wee bit fast, did he?"

When I returned to AVTEC in August of 1996 to complete my five-year renewal for radar, Dennis hadn't changed a bit. I looked around the full class of new students and all I could do was smile, knowing what those poor students had coming that week. Dennis just winked and said, "Well lad, nice to have you back. You remember what I taught ya?"

The funny thing was, I did.

After radar, the following three months at AVTEC involved classes six days a week, ten hours a day, to prepare thirty-plus students to take the Coast Guard exam. Licenses ranged from 50 ton to 100 ton inspected, and about four or five of us, including myself, were going to be sitting for a 1600 ton master and mate uninspected for fishing vessel tickets. The class consisted mostly of fishermen, but we also had charter and tourist boat people, along with a few from oil rigs and tugboats.

The instructor for this part looked like he walked out of a Hemingway novel. Clem McCann stood about 5'8" with a head full of disheveled gray hair that looked like Einstein on his worst hair day. He sported a bushy lopsided mustache that was stained yellow from the cigarettes he chain-smoked and looked to be around eighty years old. In the past he had worked at Woods Hole, Massachusetts, and had also lived in the Caribbean for quite some time before coming to Seward to teach.

Clem and his wife lived on a 40-foot sailboat docked in the small boat harbor. He'd be at his desk at 5 a.m., seven days a week, sitting in front of his computer smoking cigarettes and pounding down dark black coffee. I made it a habit to come in around 5:30 or 6 a.m. to have coffee with him and he'd spend a half hour or so every morning helping me in areas I was having difficulty with.

Each day in class Clem would hand out a stack of Coast Guard questions on worksheets for whatever subject we'd be on. At the end of the three months the booklets I saved filled up two big boxes. Clem single-handedly helped keep the pulp mills in business. He had every Coast Guard question that had ever been presented in his data bank. By the time we were through, we had looked up and answered every question ever asked by the Coasties.

Throughout the course someone would prove a Coast Guard answer to a question wrong. Clem would take great joy in faxing the Coast Guard in Washington, D.C., and informing them of their error, along with sending proof and the person's name that discovered it. I received credit for three. Clem told me over the previous six or seven years his classes had corrected over a hundred Coast Guard questions. I can imagine this frustrated the Coast Guard to no end.

There are easier schools to attend with shorter time frames and computers, but Clem felt that these schools were just teaching how to pass the test and not adequately covering the fundamentals and knowledge he felt the person holding a license should have. He wanted students to learn navigation in its purest form.

One morning over coffee, I was sitting in his office trying to stay upwind of his thick cigarette smoke. We were talking about modern day electronics and how everything we were learning was all done for us with computerization. I never forgot what he told me that morning.

"Corky, let's say you're 200 miles offshore in the Bering Sea and you're in a terrible storm. A huge wave takes out your wheelhouse windows, destroying all your fancy electronics. Your radar, radios, GPS, and depth recorders are all gone and the only thing you now have is a magnetic compass. That's all. Could you find your way back safely to the port you left from?"

I looked at him, thought about what he said, and had to admit that no, I couldn't.

"Well young man," he said, "when you leave my class and hold in your hand that piece of paper you so much desire, you will be able to find your way home. This is what I am here to teach you."

Clem is a very wise man. In 1992, I had a fire in my compressor room that knocked out all my electronics. I had to travel over 360 nautical miles from Togiak to Dutch Harbor using only a magnetic compass and a 12-volt radio. Clem taught me well. I remembered his lessons and thank him.

The three months of class came and went, but at the time it seemed like the longest, hardest period of my life. I had never applied myself in school before, and had previously had an attitude to do just enough to get by. Perhaps it had something to do with my father being a high school principal. My college days were filled with parties, hockey, skiing, and women. Anything but books and studying. That fall I learned self-discipline, good work and study habits, and how to truly apply myself to a task.

When it was time to take the Coast Guard exams I was so nervous I woke up at 4 a.m., scared to death that I would forget everything that I had spent so long learning. I just knew I was going to screw it up.

I beat Clem to school that morning. He took one look at me and knew I was an emotional mental case. He took me for a ride in his old beat up station wagon to go have a cup of coffee. He calmed me down in no time by just a few kind words and some sound advice.

The next two days I passed all six sections of the exam with the third highest score out of thirty-five students. I received my master 1600 ton uninspected license, with 100 tons inspected, and mate 200 ton inspected merchant marine license. That night we had a party at the Breeze Inn on Seward's waterfront and the whole class, including Clem, got roaring drunk. It was one of the happiest days of my life.

Ten years later, my wife, Barb, sat for basically the same 100 ton Coast Guard test. She missed a total of one question out of the entire four-part exam. Clem, I hope wherever you are you read this, ONE question. Can you believe that? Shit.

THE FACTORY TRAWLER INDUSTRY

My Start

One of the people I went to school with, John, belonged to a family that owned a couple of factory trawlers based out of Seattle. He set up a meeting for me with their company to look at one of their boats, the *Pacific Trawler*, which was a 132-foot Bender head and gut factory boat.

When I first stepped onboard the vessel it was apparent it hadn't been kept up to any real standard and looked tired. But under the dirt, piles of gear, and general disarray, I felt the boat had a lot to offer. The potential for a good platform to fish from was there.

I was taken to the Deep Sea office and introduced to the personnel, finally coming to the operations manager, John's sister. Right away I knew I'd end up butting heads with this woman. Towards me, at least, she had the personality of a sea lion. We did end up with a deal, however, and I agreed to take the vessel for the 1992 season.

I flew home for Christmas before returning to oversee the final weeks of shipyard and gear work that needed to be done before heading to the rock sole fishery that opened January 20. In winter, rock sole are egg (roe) bearing and bring a very good price in Japan, which usually averages from $1.40 to $1.80 per pound.

We were late getting all the work done, but the boat was finally loaded and ready on Friday, January 17, for sea trials, where we test all systems before heading north. To do this, we had to go through the Ballard locks of Lake Washington in Seattle. Maneuvering a factory trawler around Lake Union is kind of like I imagine driving a semi through the streets of New York City to be—very tight quarters with lots of traffic. To say I was nervous going through those locks for the first time, moving a deep draft and underpowered boat, is a vast understatement. The *Pacific Trawler* drew about 15 feet underwater and only had about 1,200 horsepower. I was scared shitless. John's father and sister were in the wheelhouse bridge with me the whole time, which made matters even worse.

I managed to do okay and didn't slam into the locks or anger the lock attendants. Although I'm an okay boat handler and feel confident I can dock just about any size vessel, even today I still get that nervous tension that seems to build in my lower spine and creep its way to a shaky hand when I have a $7 million boat in confined quarters or bad wind conditions.

As we departed Seattle for Alaska on January 18 at 2:30 a.m., we headed out through the Strait of Juan de Fuca into the Pacific Ocean, beelining for Kodiak on a crossing that was amazingly uneventful. Deck work and factory prep was completed two days before we arrived in Kodiak on January 24. We picked up the fisheries observer we were required to take from NMFS, topped off the fuel tanks, and were on our way in six hours.

Two days into the trip, we steamed smack into a winter storm like a Nor'easter while trying to make it through Unimak Pass. The wind was blowing 60 knots from the northeast and about an inch of ice was forming each hour over the entire boat while our speed crept along at 1.5 knots. It was a hellish sixteen hours. The crew was forced to bust ice in these conditions by going out in pairs, with one guy breaking ice while the other held a lifeline for him.

We finally got in the lee of Seal Cape and worked our way to a mile off the beach of Cape Sarichef, arriving in the Bering Sea at long last.

We arrived at the fishing grounds on January 27, seven days late. Most of the fishing fleet well on their way to completing their first trip while we were just getting started. Our opening day brought in about 15 tons of finished rock sole roe fish. At $1.70 a pound, 33,000 pounds brought in a day's pay of $56,000 for the vessel and netted me about $1,600. Not bad for my first day of fishing on a factory trawler. I began to think I was going to like the business.

The rock sole that are targeted every January during what is called *A* season occur in considerable numbers. The peak of the spawning season and the largest concentrations of roe fish usually occur around mid to late February. The females are quite a bit larger than the males, with an average weight of about 500 grams compared to 200 grams for the males. Back in the old days of this fishery (yes, 1992 is considered the old days) only the female rock sole were kept. All other species, except perhaps some Pacific cod and egg-bearing flathead sole, were discarded. (Today fishermen try to utilize as much of the bycatch species as possible and the percentage of overall fish retained has greatly increased.)

After the codend of the net was dumped onboard, the fish went through a sorting line where the species were separated. The egg-bearing rock soles would be cut by hand, removing the head in a V-type cut that exposes the rich reddish-pink egg sack in the body cavity without cutting the roe sack itself. If the sack is cut, the roe becomes worthless and the fish is downgraded to a No. 2 grade. Scale loss, bruising, and dark spots on the white side of the fish are all other reasons for the fish to become No. 2 grade, which is generally worth 25–40¢ less a pound.

The next step in processing is to wash and pack the sole. Each boat has its own method of doing their packs. The size of the packs will vary, but are usually 12–20 kilogram blocks. Smaller packs generally bring a little more at market but are more time consuming and labor intensive, so it's a trade-off.

After the fish is panned, the blocks are weighed and a water solution that forms a glaze is added. This helps prevent freezer burning and makes the fish pack a solid substance. Then the product is placed into big plate freezers that have vertical rows of plates that usually fit ten pans per row, with eight to twelve horizontal rows per freezer. These freezers are run on R-22 freon which operates at or below -30°F. The blocks become frozen after three or four hours and are then broken out of the pans and placed in either separate bags or two blocks to a cardboard box, depending on the vessel. They are stamped with the date, species, size of the fish (S, M, L, LL), with or without roe, and weight before being sent down into the freezer hold, located on the lowest level of the vessel.

A very accurate tally is kept of the product so the vessel knows exactly how much they produce each day and the total amount onboard at any given time. A very detailed logbook is kept in the wheelhouse on the production, discards, and the fishing activities. A yellow copy of the log is given to NMFS and the original stays onboard the vessel.

Six days after our start on the *Pacific Trawler* we had a major setback. One of our two 3408 Caterpillar generators in our engine room, which supply all the electricity onboard, threw a rod out through the side of the engine block. It looked like someone set a grenade off inside the oil pan. On one side a hole the size of a baseball was blown out and on the other half the block was gone. I have never since seen or heard of an engine coming apart this bad.

On top of losing the generator, my assistant engineer, Mark, suffered third and fourth degree burns on his left arm from his wrist to his elbow from hot oil and steam that was released when the engine blew. We wrapped him up in gauze with a half pound of burn cream and he refused to go home. I'd change his bandage every night to his cries of "No, no, not the red stuff," referring to the medicated cream I used on his wound before finishing his dressing and applying a new bandage. He was one tough man.

We couldn't freeze fish and operate the boat with only one generator, so we had to break the trip and head into Akutan, a remote island located east of Dutch Harbor that has a small Native village and a large fish processing plant. There we offloaded our product and hooked up a 400-kilowatt shaft generator to run off the main engine. We hoped this would get us by until the end of the season. What it did for sure was rob even more power from a very underpowered vessel.

We managed to finish the season this way and barely got the boat topped off when the season in Dutch Harbor closed on February 23. We finished up with 250 tons of roe fish, which was not so great compared to the fleet average, but was still the best roe season the vessel had to date.

We headed into the Gulf of Alaska and back to Kodiak to finish the end of the rock sole roe season there. The fish were on their tail end of the spawning season and we managed to get a few days in before we switched to rockfish.

Shortraker and rougheye rockfish are the largest rockfish in the Northern Pacific, with some weighing over 40 pounds. They are bright red, slow growing, and live a long time. Some are estimated to be over sixty years old. It takes about twenty years (or 5 pounds) for a shortraker to reach reproductive maturity. In 1992 we were allowed to target these amazing rockfish that live in deep water along steep edges and hard bottoms. They are not easy to catch, but sure are a lot of fun.

All rockfish species have an air swim bladder that expands radically when the fish are brought up from the deep. When the bladders fill up, the fish float and you know before the codend comes onboard that you're in them. You see a great white charge of bubbles foaming way back in your wake and the codend comes shooting out of the water like a nuclear submarine during an emergency surfacing. Once at the surface, a monstrous high-floating tube of red trails behind. I've actually had bags "blow" to the surface while I was still hauling my doors in, with over 50 fathoms (300 feet) of wire left to haul up.

Today there is a lot of controversy about the health of red rockfish stocks, including shortrakers and rougheyes. Scientists claim populations are down, but a number of fishermen disagree, including me. I know of a lot of areas where these and other species of rockfish are more abundant than ever before. I'd love to have the opportunity to prove these statistics but, as in many fields, the real experts on certain matters are the last ones to be consulted.

Most studies on fisheries are done either with National Oceanic and Atmospheric Association (NOAA) ships or with fishing boats that have a scientist onboard. In both cases, they tow in certain areas and when they don't find the fish they are after the fish is often labeled as in a decline and the fishery is shut down. I think if they moved twenty miles and looked in the proper depth, millions of pounds of the declining species would be found.

It is the feeling of some fishermen like me that the studies done by NOAA and other research ships are a complete joke. These vessels are usually not trawlers, most of their captains are not fishermen, and their deckhands don't have a clue about tuning trawl gear. It would be like me doing spotted owl surveys. This same problem also exists on the Atlantic coast. Scientists there say bluefin tuna have declined, yet the fishermen know there are now more than ever. It's a battle.

Our red rockfish trip ended in 1992 with the closure of the Gulf of Alaska on March 24. We had a week off before it opened again on April 1 for the second quarter. I flew home to finish the ski season in Girdwood and take some time off.

I was called back during the first part of May and arrived in Dutch Harbor to find four guys from the Faeroe Islands onboard, including my mate, two engineers, and a deckhand. More lost Vikings. While I was home the company decided to sell part of the vessel to these guys and I had their countrymen for crew. The mate couldn't speak a speck of English and yet I was supposed to leave this guy alone in the wheelhouse for eight hours. He wouldn't be able to answer the radio if another vessel needed to work out a passing situation or talk to the American crew on deck. There was no way I was going to go along with the situation. At the fuel dock the two engineers were drunk and planning to pump 40,000 gallons into tanks that held around 20,000. They were having a small problem of liters versus gallons. I stopped the operation before we had a fuel spill on our hands and went to the Coast Guard, turned in these illegal immigrants, and called the sea lion (owner of the company) and told her to stuff it. It led to her partners being deported—as soon as they got out of jail, that is. I was boatless once more.

THE *GOLDEN FLEECE*

I was home a week when I received a call from John Henderschedt of Golden Age Fisheries in Seattle. They needed someone to skipper the *Golden Fleece*, a small head and gut factory boat. My old partner from the JV days, Richard McLellan, was working for them running the *Linda Rose* and the two of us were reunited.

The *Golden Fleece* was one of the smallest factory trawlers operating at the time. At 104 feet long, over 30 feet wide, and with a draft (overall depth) of over 13 feet, it was a big little boat. It had twin 700 horsepower Caterpillar main engines with 6-inch shafts swinging over 60-inch square propellers. This boat had a lot of power and was a small but mighty towing machine.

We had bunks for fourteen people, two big 120-pan freezers, and deck and wheelhouse machinery that would make a lot of larger vessels envious. Up until this point, it was the finest towing boat I'd had the pleasure to operate and I quickly fell in love with it.

I flew into Dillingham, Alaska, and took a floatplane out to Togiak Bay where the *Golden Fleece* was fishing with the fleet for yellowfin sole. The chief engineer, deckhand, cook, and I were taken out to the vessel by a leaky zodiac with the deckhand madly pumping away with a foot pump to keep us from sinking.

Togiak Bay is a wonderful place to be in early summer. The male walruses all hole up on nearby Round Island, which now had a twelve-mile no entry zone around it so the walruses can have a quiet environment to sunbathe in. The only people allowed in this zone are Alaska natives who shoot these sleeping monsters and take their teeth and tusks. I think the walruses would prefer the draggers.

Yellowfin sole are the most abundant flatfish species in the Bering Sea. Marketable yellowfin range from 250 to 700 grams. They are found in depths of three fathoms (18 feet) in Togiak, and range to depths over 450 feet throughout the Bering Sea. There are some small pockets where they occur in the Gulf of Alaska, but in far fewer numbers.

The largest problem with fishing for yellowfin is they aren't worth much, netting about $500 per metric ton or 22¢ a pound in the round (whole). We can usually get around $700 a ton if we head and gut them (31¢ a pound), but this is really labor intensive. Yellowfin is a volume fishery and you have to be set up to run volume and get a lot through the factory to make money at this game.

On the *Golden Fleece* this would not happen with only fourteen people onboard. The most we could do was seven freezers a day at 840 pans of fish weighing 17 kilos each (or 14.3 metric tons). This worked out to a $7,140 boat gross. The boat held 100 tons of product, making the total load worth $50,000 for a seven-day trip. When you figure in expenses such as fuel, food, insurance, crew, packaging, travel expenses, gear, lube oil, parts for the factory, engine room costs, and refrigeration for even a small factory rig, at 22¢ a pound you're not going to come out very far ahead.

Factory personnel hate yellowfin sole. They work like dogs and don't make very much money. The crew share for one of these $50,000 seven-day trips would be around $400 to a guy who worked sixteen hours a day for seven days. That's $57 a day, or about $3.50 an hour.

So here we were towing in the shallows for yellowfin, hating it and wishing that we were fishing for anything else. While getting fuel for the boat on the second day every alarm on the electric panel went off and the boat went dark. The electronics fizzled and then went out. The gyrocompass was going around in circles like it was possessed. I grabbed a flashlight and ran down into the engine room, where I met the engineer, Jim, on his way out.

"Fire in the compressor room" he yelled, and we both grabbed CO2 extinguishers. Within a minute we had dumped about 20 pounds of CO2 in the Sabroe refrigeration panel while holding our breath. Once the fire was out we backed off and I helped Jim into a Scott air pack firefighting unit and sent him back into the compressor room.

The whole refrigeration panel was history, but not before sending a voltage shock wave throughout the entire vessel. Our steering was out except for a manual wheel and the electronics had only a 12-volt system still operational. This included a VHF radio, Loran, and weather fax. We had over 300 miles to go to reach Dutch Harbor with hand steering and no radar.

We arrived in Dutch three days later and very frazzled. It took two days at the dock to put us back together. A POP fishery opening saved us from having to do yellowfin again and we made our way west to a deepwater edge off the Pribilof Islands.

After our third tow for POP the port door slipped down out of the ballard. My mate went to suck it back up to the block and—pow!—the main wire parted, sending our Thyboron trawl door to the bottom. Back to Dutch we went again. All I could think was how do you like me so far Golden Age?

After ten days I'd made a total of eleven tows, blew stuff up, melted $40,000 worth of Sabroe refrigeration circuits, lost a $10,000 trawl door, and burned about 15,000 gallons of diesel for about $5,000 worth of fish. I better turn this little spell of bad luck around and quick, or I'd be pumping gas at Mapco and talking about bad luck.

An O-flats fishery opened up third quarter on July 1 that included flatfish such as flathead sole and rock sole. We started this fishery off with some quick seven-day trips offloading in St. Paul in the Pribilof Islands. By August 15, we had six successful trips in when the season closed on us. I could finally breathe a sigh of relief.

I went home to fly fish the Kenai River and tramp around the mountains looking for a Dall ram. I did well on the rainbows but a ram eluded me, as they do every year I try to hunt them. I've never shot one and am starting to think I probably never will.

I returned to finish off the season in October. This is usually the time of year when most of the money shots are over and the weather turns really bad in the Bering Sea and Gulf of Alaska. Boats, gear, and crew are all worn out from the year's drive. It seems like the engineers and captains can only think about getting to the shipyard and having their boats fixed and prepared for the next season. The companies, on the other hand, want to squeeze that last dollar out of the final season of the year before checks have to be written by the owners to the shipyard and twine companies.

The fall season of 1992 was a gamble that paid off for us. We started targeting rock sole and stumbled across some rex sole migrating either out or into Shelikof Strait. We were the first to find these $1 a pound sole and fished for six weeks, making a nice living.

Towards the end word got out and three or four boats found us. Today just about the whole fleet knows about this fall fishery and the fish aren't there in the same numbers as before. But I'll always remember that fall. The weather was terrible and it seemed like it blew a 100 knots every day, but the fishing was incredible.

As the first week of November rolled around, the deepwater flatfish season closed and we found ourselves with no other lucrative fisheries available. We called it a season and pounded our way back across a stormy Gulf of Alaska towards Seattle and the shipyard.

This small boat engraved even further into me the high grading formula of fishing, along with dishonest (flat out lying) fishing practices. Running the boat versus the laws I was supposed to follow were two totally different things. The boat only held 100 metric tons of fish, so we put up the best product with the highest value we could in order to maximize the trip. The rest went overboard, dead or alive, but I didn't care. I was playing the game.

A BAD TRIP NORTH

The Inside Passage

When traveling back to Alaska from the shipyards in Seattle, most boats will take the Inside Passage through Canada's protected waters into Southeastern Alaska. They either come out at the Dixon entrance near Prince Rupert, Canada, or Icy Straits, west of Juneau, Alaska. This route allows crews to get their boats squared away and to finish last minute gear work, store gear away, and fine-tune the factory equipment, all in the comfort of being out of the weather. Depending on how far north the boat goes, the route can last up to five days.

The problem with the Inside Passage is there are a few really weird passages affected by huge tides, strong currents, and tricky channels. The place is crowded with everything from tugboats and barges to freighters, log booms, ferries, cruise ships, pleasure yachts, and small boats. I couldn't just turn on the autopilot, pick up a good book, and glance at the radar in-between pages. You have to pay attention all the time.

A great feature of this route, however, is from the time you depart Ballard in Seattle and you check in with vessel services, they hand you off to different stations all along the way until you depart Canadian waters. For a good portion of this route they have you on radar and track your progress. They let you know who your oncoming and overtaking traffic is, the estimated time of arrival of such vessels, and anything else to worry about such as lost logs or bad squalls. Traffic keeps you informed and you have a series of check-in points throughout the route. It's a great aid to navigation and is extremely well set up. I wish Southeast Alaska also had this service.

Our trip north in 1993 was uneventful until we entered Alaskan waters. We were near the Dixon entrance to start our journey across the Gulf of Alaska, but had about one more day of gear work to finish. I decided to continue up the Inside Passage to Icy Straits. We had better than a week to go before the fishery opening, with nothing but time.

The Wrangle Narrows is a twelve mile or so channel that weaves through rocks, islands, sandbars, and ledges to the town of St. Petersburg, Alaska. I'm sure the locals know the narrows like their own living room, but I don't. I only pass through there two times a year, at most.

The place is well-marked with stationary and floating buoys, but at night the buoys all blend together and it's hard to distinguish which ones are the next in the series. The one time I went through this place at night, it was a nightmare.

This year we jogged around at the southern entrance, waiting a couple of hours for first light, and didn't start entering the passage until 7:30 a.m. The tides dictated dead low water at 8:20 a.m. It wasn't the best time to go, but at least it was light out.

The narrow channel is about thirty feet wide in the narrowest part and opens up to about a quarter mile or more in other areas. It's tight. Unlike today when we have C-plot and electronic charts which put the whole channel on a computer screen and lists the buoys, taking all the guesswork out of it, we had to navigate manually. I had my mate on the wheel, with a deckhand calling out buoy numbers to me. I stood at the fishing station watching our depth sounders and radar, and plotting our course through the narrows.

We went by a small Coast Guard buoy tender as we started into the channel. About two-thirds of the way through we passed a floating green can buoy about forty or fifty feet off our port side when—wham!—the port side of the boat lurched about two feet in the air and then settled right back down. We were doing about 9 knots and whatever we hit, we hit hard. I had my face in the radar and looked over to the depth sounder, which read twelve feet of water under the keel. I had no idea what we had hit.

The engineer, Jim, called up that the engine room was flooding and the port engine was starting to overheat. I pitched and clutched out the port main engine, thus taking it out of gear, while Jim secured the engine room and stopped the water coming in from the keel cooler. We idled the rest of the way to Petersburg, Alaska, where the harbor master found us at a dock. As far as we could figure, we had hit the mooring anchor (which is probably a huge cement block) when we passed the green can.

I found it strange that a buoy tender was in the area and told the Coast Guard I thought the buoy was off station when they came down to inspect the accident. It was a bad move. Never blame the government for any incident, even if you feel you are right. They are masters at covering for themselves and shifting the blame to you.

The Coast Guard sent a tender to check the buoy. I was told it was where it was supposed to be and they said they doubted if I hit their anchor set up. I hit bottom, according to them, and they wrote me up.

The shore engineer, Greg, flew in with an underwater welder and we found the keel cooler crushed, but no other damage. We had to cut the cooler loose, cap off the through hulls, and install a heat exchanger for a cooling system for the port main engine. We were finished and fixed up in three days, but now time was everything and I'd be late for the season's opening.

Three days later we were outside of Kodiak when a major winter storm struck, blowing northeast 60 knots and making a lot of ice on our surface areas. Here we go again, fighting the clock and a storm shows up to really let us know we're late. It slowed us way down to 1.5–3 knots.

We began beating and breaking up the ice every two hours and then around the clock in shifts to keep up with it. This went on for two days until we finally got in the lee of Unimak Island and into the Bering Sea. Was I ever going to show up on time to start a new year?

We arrived in Dutch Harbor on the morning of January 23. Bill Sage, the operations manager for Golden Age Fisheries, met us at the dock, relieved that we were still alive. The boat had been so iced up that the communication dome became inoperable and we couldn't transmit out on the radio due to the ice on the antennae. No one had heard from us in three days.

Although the 1993 season started out bad, the overall season was good and we had a good gross stock. The fishing industry, especially the factory trawling industry, was going through major changes, which it continues to go through today. Boats were going from one owner to another and companies were forming and folding every year. It seemed that the boats remained the same; they just rotated under new management.

This was also a year of change for Golden Age Fisheries. They began the year with five boats and finished with two. Sadly, the *Golden Fleece* was one of the three to be sold. I didn't find out about the sale until December, when it was too late to find another boat for the 1994 *A* season that runs from late January into March, one of two lucrative groundfish seasons for the year.

With no job in sight, I collected unemployment and skied a lot that winter, putting in over a hundred days on the ski slopes. I lived off savings, credit cards, and moose meat, and had a great winter while I spent my life's savings and went into debt.

In April of 1994 I received a call from a fishing acquaintance, Mike Green. He was forming a new company and planned to buy a boat with two partners. We talked about different boats that were available and agreed to look into a smaller factory trawler that was repossessed by the bank.

By May, a deal was made with the bank and ScanSea Investment, Ltd., was formed. A 140-foot factory trawler, *Continuity*, was purchased. I had another boat. It was a good thing because the moose meat was just about gone, the credit cards were maxed, and the ski season was ending in a week.

THE *PROSPERITY*

A First Trip from Hell

I arrived in Ballard in May of 1994 to find the *Continuity* hauled out at Tipper shipyard. For years I'd seen the boat in different forms. While the vessel was now 140 feet long, 31 feet wide, and drew 10 feet under the water, it started its life as a 90-foot vessel, built somewhere in the South. It had been used as a scallop fishing vessel, a trawler, and maybe even a crabber. It had switched owners and names like most people change underwear.

Once again the *Continuity* was going through another metamorphosis. This time she was renamed the *Prosperity* and became a head and gut factory trawler. It should have dawned on me that when a boat jumps from owner to owner, it's because it doesn't ever make any money. Something big time is wrong somewhere in the scheme of things. Today, I'd take one look at the *Prosperity* and shake with fear. The last time I saw it, the boat was tied to a reposition dock on Lake Washington, rusting away. But in 1994, to my shorebound soul it looked like a beautiful Caddie. I was sure I could make a lot of money with it, and told the owners so.

The three partners of ScanSea, Ltd., Carsten, Dave, and Mike, put their life savings into this boat. They had mortgaged their homes and borrowed from banks, Japanese fish buyers, and anyone else they could get a buck from. Somehow they came up with enough money for the boat, along with enough working capital to do some shipyard work and to buy some gear. To say we were operating on a shoestring budget would be describing the situation mildly. These guys cried poverty from the moment I met them and this was their tune for as long as I was associated with them, no matter how many fish we were able to catch and how much money we made.

Reality started to sink in almost immediately. With the boat hauled out at the shipyard, I was amazed at how little of the vessel there was under the water line. It had a very shallow draft and flat bottom, with not much of a keel. The twin screw wheels of the propeller were very small, with 55-inch squares and 4-inch shafts. In comparison, the *Golden Fleece*, which was around two-thirds the size of the *Prosperity*, had 6-inch shafts with over 65 inches of variable pitch props. At least the *Prosperity* had nozzles, which are tubes that surround the propeller and direct more water through the propeller blades, thus creating more thrust from the blades. This alone would increase the bollard pull (power) by 15 percent or more.

The boat had a fairly high bow with a nice flare, which I did like. The huge bulbous bow could be tanked down and filled with water for ballast when needed. Above the water line it was tall with total shelter decks from the deck level to eight feet and higher. This was nice for the deckhands, but gave the vessel a huge surface area, which would work against us in windy conditions.

Rapp Hydema, a company that makes winches, net reels, forward sweep winches, and pull masters for pulling and lifting, manufactured all the deck machinery. The long, wide trawl deck had a roomy bosun's locker for the deckhands, which was particularly nice.

The wheelhouse was an aluminum structure with good visibility. The electronics had been almost all stolen, so we had some insurance money to use for updating and replacing missing units. This was good because I was able to spend this money where I wanted it and put in the machines of my choice.

For the next four weeks I worked for free while helping to get the boat ready to head north. The worst possible thing you can do to a fishing vessel in the factory trawler business is to let it sit idle for a year. This combined with years of bad upkeep and neglect made the rig in need of a complete overhaul. Spare parts were nonexistent and money was tight. We had to fix the most important and obvious problems and hope for the best in the other areas.

The two full-time engineers and one shore engineer the company had hired were a major problem from the start. I'll just refer to them as Mutt and Jeff, and I'll call the shore engineer Basil. I worked with some real winners on this boat, and I'm afraid if I use their real names they'll burn my house down, or worse.

Mutt and Jeff would do as little as possible. Between the two, they knew just about enough to get themselves a job in the industry. Add the two together and you have one bad engineer. The shore engineer was from India, knew nothing about the fishing industry, and should have been deported. I don't think India would have allowed him back into their country, however. They probably hate guys like him too. Anyway, these three guys would soak the new owners for hours supposedly worked, complain about the work, fight with me on projects, and spend more time in the bars than on the boat. They were totally incompetent and in way over their heads.

I put in a call to an engineer I had worked with at Golden Age Fisheries. Bob Carter had given his notice to Golden Age and said he'd be interested if the pay was right, but that he wouldn't be available until September, since during the summers he runs a blueberry farm in Maine. Bob is what I consider one of the best engineers in the business, so I made sure the owners agreed to pay Bob his asking price of $300 a day in guaranteed wages. This was more than my own guarantee of $250 a day. Bob agreed to come to work for us in September and I hoped and prayed Mutt and Jeff wouldn't sink us until the berries were ripe.

The boat was finally together enough to do a series of sea trials, where we gave the boat a good rundown, including swinging the compass and testing everything but the net reels and main winches. This was a big time bad move that would later come back to haunt us.

We departed Seattle on July 14, 1994, at 6 p.m. with a freshly painted boat. At least we looked good. After eight hours I turned in and handed the helm over to Mike Green, one of the owners who was making the first trip with us. I remember feeling fairly good that night. It was the last good night's sleep I'd have for quite some time.

The next day the horror show began. I awoke, made a latte, and had no sooner sat in my chair in the wheelhouse when the autopilot that we were using to steer the ship quit. I dropped the steaming cup of coffee on my lap as I tried to reach for the manual controls of the boat. With a very important part of my anatomy feeling like a lobster that's been dropped into a boiling pot, I crumbled to the floor screaming.

The boat listed 25 degrees in a hard-over turn while traveling at 10 knots of speed in the Straits of Juan de Fuca, the shipping channel used between Washington and Canada. What seemed like a hundred pleasure boats, sailboats, tugboats, and barges scattered to all points of the compass to get out of the way of a possessed factory trawler doing donuts in the shipping lanes.

I finally picked myself up, holding my pile pants away from my burnt manhood, and hauled back on the twin throttles to bring the boat to an idle. By this time I had almost the entire crew rushing into the wheelhouse, wondering if their captain had lost his mind. There I stood, holding my crotch with one hand while cursing like crazy and trying to untangle myself from the wheelhouse chair. Mike Green slept through the entire ordeal.

Traffic control for the area watched the whole scene on radar and called to ask me what I was doing and to inform me I was now in the separation zone, a strip of water that separates north and southbound traffic. I managed to get the boat back in the correct shipping lane by using manual steering and to find the cause for why the gyro compass was doing circles at Mach 1 speed.

Less than twenty-four hours out and our autopilot and compass were out. This meant we'd have to hand steer the beast 1,200 miles to Kodiak. At least we had the magnetic compass swung during the sea trials in Seattle. This thought no sooner enters my mind than one of the steel balls from the compass falls off the mounting and rolls across the wheelhouse floor. The guy who had swung the compass during our shipyard work was about eighty years old and tightening the nut that held the ball in place must have slipped his mind. Our psycho bat turns must have knocked it free. Now our magnetic compass was just about useless. All I could think of was, what next?

Steering across the Gulf of Alaska while 500 miles offshore without a compass is like driving a jeep across the desert with only the North Star to guide your way while you're trying to head west. With only our GPS pointing the way, our track going across the plotter was zigzagging on a course that probably rivaled the kind of course the old Liberty ships of World War II would have taken to make themselves a hard target for German subs.

Mike, three deckhands, and I took shifts of two to four hours at a time to steer as we fishtailed our way across the Gulf of Alaska for six days. It entailed 144 hours of mind-numbing navigation before arriving at Portlock Bank, located fifty miles off Kodiak Island. Since the Gulf of Alaska is open to trawling and we were in the Gulf, we decided to fish and proceeded to set the net.

On July 20 at 8 p.m., we set out our brand new 440 trawl net in 130 fathoms (780 feet) of water southeast of Portlock Bank, targeting rex sole. Everything went surprisingly smooth and two hours later we hauled back 40 tons of POP, sablefish (black cod), and 100 pounds of rex sole. The only problem was the law reads I can only have 20 percent of my round weight equivalent of POP and sablefish against my target species of rex sole. This put me a tad bit over my by catch limit and by law I was supposed to run it all overboard. What I did instead was decide to run it all through the factory, figuring I'd catch enough rex sole in the next few tows to make it up.

We set out the next tow in 80 fathoms (480 feet). The doors settled, I punched in tow mode on the Rapp computerized trawl system, and the main winches started peeling out one-inch diameter main wire in a free spool at about 300 rpm. This created a tangled mess like a bird's nest on the spools of the drums. I kicked the boat out of gear and everything became tight. The winches made very unhealthy slamming noises and took out both wire counter transponders. Luckily, the safety couplings didn't go out and the haul-in mode still worked manually. We wound the wire back on top of the tangle, put our net on the reel, and hand-steered our way to Kodiak, madly sending faxes to the Rapp guys.

I called down to the factory and told the crew to throw over the fish they had begun to run through the factory, since it looked like we weren't going to have those rex soles quite yet and weren't supposed to keep the fish.

Ed Ramburg from Hydro Pro and Andy from Alaska Hydraulics both came out on July 24 to try to figure out our winch problems in Kodiak. During the sea trials they held, the winches went into free spool, repeating the same effect again. Mutt and Jeff slept through the sea trials and didn't seem to be concerned. Six hours later, with some hydraulic magic, the problem was figured out and cured. I have no clue what these guys did or what they installed, tweaked, or did otherwise, but the winches worked when they were done.

I was especially hoping we'd get the autopilot going before we departed town, but it just wasn't going to happen. We fixed what we could and departed Kodiak on July 27, hoping our problems were behind us. By July 30, we had started to get things working. Bugs were found and either put on a list, which seemed to suit Mutt and Jeff best, or fixed, patched up, or band-aided together. We began to catch a few fish and slowly started to put a trip together.

By the end of the week, I decided to run offshore and make a couple of tows in 300 fathoms to fill our bycatch of thorny head rockfish, which are commonly called idiots. We had yet to fish that deep and in hindsight I should have paid better attention to what Elies from Dantrawl told me back in June in Seattle. He said the previous owner had put new main wire on top of very old cable that he had left on the drum for filler. While still in Seattle we started to pull the main wire off to check it out. When we came to a C-splice at the 500-fathom mark, the wire beneath was brand new and it looked like there was another 300–400 fathoms of wire still on the drum. I didn't go any further and concluded Elies was mistaken as we wound the wire back onto the winch.

Now in the Gulf of Alaska, we arrived at the edge of the fishing grounds and started setting gear. For 300 fathoms of water I punched in 750 fathoms of cable to reach a two-and-a-half-to-one ratio. Since we didn't have an autopilot or autotrawl, we had to have a deckhand in the wheelhouse setting the doors manually while I steered the boat to keep us on course. As Chris, the deckhand, came to 700 fathoms he called out "splice" for a second time, after already calling our splice at 500 fathoms. The second calling of splice set off a warning buzz in my brain.

"Chris, didn't you already come to a splice?"

"Yeap, that's a second one," he replied, shrugging.

I slowed the boat down to an idle and told Chris to stop the winches. I ran out to the trawl deck to check the condition of the wire. As soon as Chris released the handles and the tension was taken on the main wires, both sides let go with two loud bangs. I was six feet from the starboard winch and watched as the ends of the wires went out through the bollards. Shit. I flew back to the wheelhouse to get a mark (latitude and longitude position) on my gear.

About 150 fathoms of rotten, rusted, and useless cable remained on the drums. All my main wires, doors, mud gear, and a brand new net with a $20,000 headrope, were now 300 fathoms (1,800 feet) below the surface on an edge about as steep as a double black diamond ski slope. All in all, it represented about $70,000 worth of gear.

"Holy suffering bat shit, Chris go wake up Mike and tell him what you just did," I said.

Next we headed back to Kodiak to buy 500 fathoms of 7/8-inch wire to build a grapple to try and retrieve the gear, but also to have a couple of shots of Jack Daniels. We wound the new cable on the starboard winch, took all the anchor chain off our anchor winch, hooked up our newly purchased grapple, and steamed back to where the gear was lost. This process took just under 48 hours.

By this time you can imagine the shape poor Mike is in. He is really wondering what he put his life's savings into. The crew is about ready to puke, quit, and start drinking heavily. Me, I'm shell-shocked.

Once back to the site of our lost gear, our wireless headrope transducer began sending a signal to the Furuno fishfinder and, thanks to the marks and plot, we had a good spot on the gear. The best we could hope for would be to grab one end of the main wire.

We proceeded to put out the grapple on the end of our marks closest to the point where the cables broke. Well I'll be damned if we weren't able to actually grab the cable about 30 fathoms from the end, catching it on the first pass. We had a fifty-fifty chance to guess what side the cable belonged on. We picked the port side and hooked the grapple to the port winch. The first thing we saw was the port door, followed by winding the net up on the aft reel. We unhooked the bridles and used the forward reel to bring the starboard side mud gear onboard, after which the starboard door broke the surface. The starboard side wire went back on its winch and we were back in business with nothing tangled, missing, or torn up. Holy Moly, maybe, just maybe, our luck was starting to change.

We finally got the first trip behind us and offloaded our fish on August 14. I made Mutt and Jeff's lives so miserable, as they did in return to me, that they quit on the last day of the trip. I don't think I've ever been happier to have anyone quit as those two guys. Having them quit also saved the company from having to pay their airfare back to Seattle, which would have been the case if I had fired them.

My engineer of choice, Bob Carter, was still freezing blueberries in Maine and couldn't come for another two weeks. We needed an engineer and assistant engineer. We found a good assistant named Ryan, a young man in his early twenties with Irish heritage, but the chief engineer we came up with was bad news. I'll call this guy Burnt, since he was clearly burnt out before he even stepped foot onboard. Ryan, however, would be with me throughout my entire 2-1/2 years with the *Prosperity*, earning his chief's license during the summer of 1996 and becoming one of the youngest chief engineers in the business.

With a better engineering department onboard, our second trip went a lot smoother. Ryan ended up working eighteen to twenty hours a day fixing Mutt and Jeff's three months worth of screwed up machinery. He was knocking items off the list every day and the boat started to function and survive a day's fishing without a major breakdown. We were still hand steering the boat, however, and this was getting old.

I began sending nasty-gram telex messages to the main office in Seattle every day regarding the need for an autopilot and a new gyrocompass. I was told it would mean two to three days at the dock to install the system and the company couldn't afford the down time. They needed the cash flow and some trips had to be made or the whole venture was going to be a bust, with the bank repossessing the vessel before the summer ended. We were under the gun.

I felt my future reputation as a fisherman was at stake. My strong competitive drive, quite likely doubled by all the years spent playing hockey as a youth, was boiling over. If I had to bend the rules a little further, so be it. With blinders on, I was now so far down a dark path I didn't think for a second it would someday catch up to me. I did what I thought had to be done.

PROSPERITY PROSPERS

At the start of trip two on the *Prosperity*, NMFS put a woman named Katy onboard as our fisheries observer. Katy was a professional observer and very good at her job. Nothing would get by this woman. Unfortunately, the trip in August of 1994 was my worst two weeks of fishing in terms of bycatch numbers. I caught one third of the halibut quota for the fleet by myself and the Gulf of Alaska fishing season closed two weeks earlier than expected due to the halibut numbers being caught.

I was fishing extremely dirty in terms of bycatch, but did very well on my rex sole numbers and making a good day's pay. I felt as if I didn't have a choice. The company needed a big shot of money if it was going to survive.

Katy would update me daily on my bycatch numbers and I'd cringe and tell her I'd move, but I wouldn't go too far. I couldn't leave the good production. This was the only time in my fishing career when I fished dirty and didn't take measures to clean it up by either leaving the area or by making gear changes.

Katy was way too sharp to even think of trying to pre-sort halibuts by throwing them overboard before she had a chance to see them. It was a practice we were still fine-tuning. You never knew where she was going to turn up. Besides, there were too many halibut in the tows. Even if we tried to remove them when she wasn't looking, it wouldn't have made much of a difference.

I later had to answer to NMFS enforcement about those two weeks and did not look forward to trying to explain my reasons. Nonetheless, trip two was very good and filled the boat with about $300,000 worth of fish. We finished the trip at the end of August, just as the season closed.

We now had operating money coming in and spent the last three days of August in Kodiak installing a new gyrocompass and autopilot, fixing our hydraulic problems, and finding cures to problem areas throughout the boat. Next we steamed three days to the Bering Sea to fish for yellowfin sole. The ride through Shumigan Pass with my new Robertson autopilot and Sperry gyrocompass was an immense pleasure. For the first time in two months I wasn't fishtailing across the water. Things were definitely looking up.

We put in two quick yellowfin sole trips in the Bering Sea before the Gulf of Alaska season opened back up for the fourth quarter of fishing on October 1. Before leaving Dutch Harbor we switched over the sole footropes on the nets to prepare for harder bottom fishing in the Gulf of Alaska. We put the hard bottom frames back on the nets and back-loaded enough supplies for two trips.

Our observer, Katy, was assigned to another vessel and we were all extremely sad to see her go, even though she was tough regarding the NMFS rules. She was like one of the crew and everyone liked her. When I saw the replacement observer, however, I forgot Katy in an instant. Wow. This woman was a knockout. I couldn't believe the Feds were putting her on my boat. Those were my first thoughts when I met Barbara Gimlin, the woman who would eventually become my wife.

For the next two days while we steamed our way to Kodiak, I followed Barb around the boat like a lovesick puppy. I would hand her a cup of latte frequently just for an excuse to talk to her. She asked if she could paint some marks on the trawl deck to help her get codend measurements and my answer was, "Hell yes, you betcha. Here, have a latte." I called the whole deck crew to help her. I would have let her paint marks on my wheelhouse if she wanted.

During the next two weeks as Barb and I got to know each other we discovered we both had similar dreams and goals. The only major difference between us was that I very much wanted a family while Barb didn't want children and was set on a dream to sail around the world. I worked very hard on this one minor little obstacle and finally convinced her that children would fit into what were fast becoming *our* dreams and goals. The sailing idea sounded okay, and why not have children to take along on the adventure and let the world be their school?

The trip and our time together at sea came to an end in mid-October. I was getting off after 5-1/2 months of very hard times in the shipyard and at sea. I was tired and needed a break. We spent two wonderful days together in Kodiak before I boarded a plane to Anchorage and she returned to the *Prosperity* to finish the last two weeks of her contract as a fisheries observer. I waited at home in Girdwood for her to finish up.

When Barb finally showed up in Girdwood during the first week of November, we made plans to go to Europe skiing for a month in December. We came to regard this as our honeymoon. Our daughter, Dancia, was conceived as we made these plans and I asked her if she would marry me. Ah, observers. You gotta love them. Who else but a fisherman and a federal employee would first fall in love while fishing, second conceive a child, third go to Europe on a honeymoon, and then finally get married the following fall.

While Barb and I were in Italy, *Prosperity* spent the time in a shipyard in Seattle getting a large portion of the bugs worked out. Our engineer, Bob, had managed to get the boat in probably the best shape the rig had ever been in. We flew back from Europe on January 1 and within a few days I was back on the boat on my way to Alaska for the 1995 *A* fishing season in the Bering Sea for rock sole.

After sitting out the 1994 *A* season, I was looking forward to the roe season. The need to make some money for the company and myself was critical. My plans were to fish until mid or late May and then take the summer off to be with Barb when the baby was due. We also had to move her from Washington to Alaska and figured that being seven months pregnant was the cut-off for her to make the drive north.

The observing company that contracted her work for NMFS surprisingly asked her to go back to work, even though she was pregnant and admitted I was the father. We both ended up working in Dutch Harbor that winter, with Barb assigned to a shore plant after a brief stint on a smaller shore-based boat that made her sick all the time due to the pregnancy. We got to see each other around every ten days when I brought the *Prosperity* in to offload fish and re-supply the boat.

The rest of *A* season went okay, even though we still had some boat problems. We ended up with three full trips during the roe season, putting in just over 300 metric tons of roe fish. The price was good and averaged around $1.80 a pound, making our gross just over a million dollars for the first two months. This gave the company its much-needed capital and helped us over the edge. Unfortunately, things didn't continue that way.

In early March, with the rock sole fishery over, I made the decision to head into the Gulf of Alaska to fish for rex sole. The weather that spring was some of the worst I'd ever seen off Kodiak. It blew hard just about every day. If it was blowing a gale of 40-knot winds with 15-foot seas, it was nice out. The rex sole were very hard to find with the weather so bad and we did a lot of damage to our gear. We seemed to trade twine for fish, and I lost two nets that March. I did manage to retrieve one; a four-seam combination trawl net with a 30-ton codend worth about $40,000, but it was destroyed.

Near the end of the month we were fishing near the south end of Portlock Bank and bringing in about 15 metric tons of rex sole with roe. It was our best production so far for the month. We were on the second day on a body of fish when a telex came through that our factory foreman's mother had died from a heart attack at fifty years old. I broke off the trip and took the guy in.

Twenty-four hours later we were back to the same area, trying to relocate the sole. That night the wind came on from the northeast at 60 knots. It was cold and a couple inches of ice quickly began to build up on the rails and deck surfaces every hour from the sea spray. Crew shifts now included additional duties to break up the ice with baseball bats, shovels, and whatever else was handy. A one-inch layer of ice on the boat can add thousands of pounds overall and seriously threaten our stability, especially on the *Prosperity*.

The icing was just the start of our problems. One of the most frequently asked questions I get from people is about the dangers they hear about fishing in general. I usually tell them the story about what happened next.

We were hauling back the last tow before dark and had 10 fathoms (60 feet) of main wire out before the trawl doors broke the surface. With the wind blowing a screaming gale, we ended up pointed downwind. The seas were building to fifteen feet and the surge was incredible just before the doors appeared. The starboard main engine died first and within seconds the port main engine also went quiet. I stopped the main winches and put the control levers to the main engine in neutral while Bob ran for the engine room to restart the main engines.

With the main engines back online, I slipped the gears into forward and both engines immediately died again. Both screws (propellers) had been fouled, but with what? Our own gear? We dead-sticked the doors up to the stern, steering with no forward power and at the mercy of the weather, tides, and waves. This was followed by bringing the ground gear and net up while drifting downwind in order to keep the gear behind us and trying to get everything onboard.

I can remember feeling greatly relieved that we were able to get the gear onboard safely, but while it was behind us it acted like a sea anchor and kept the stern of the boat pointed into the wind. With the gear now onboard but the rudders and props still fouled, we were soon broadside to treacherous seas. Things got ugly quick and we were getting nailed.

Bob re-started the main engines and we tried reverse, hoping to kick whatever it was out using the forward force of the nozzles. Most large trawlers have nozzles that are large tapered cones that surround the propeller blades. The nozzles are slightly smaller in diameter on the aft end, and the clearance between the blades of the props and the inside surface of each nozzle is about an inch. The water is forced through the nozzle and creates a great thrust for the prop.

The engines died again as soon as the props tried to turn. Whatever we had fouled, it was really stuck and was not going to come out. By this time we decided we were really screwed.

It was blowing at least 70 knots by now and the tops of the 20-foot seas were being blown flat. This happens in a major storm, where a steady wall of water is blown across the tops of the swells. I had to call the Coast Guard for help for the first time in my life.

Calls to the Coast Guard are made over the single side band radio at 4125 kilohertz. As soon as the connection is made, the whole fishing world knows you're in trouble. All boats monitor 4125 and when a boat is in trouble the Coast Guard puts out a pan-pan every fifteen minutes, which means very important message. The message that day was about the *Prosperity*.

I hung my head in shame as I went through the standard half-hour question and answer session with a radio operator at the Coast Guard station in Kodiak who sounded like she was from the deep South. At the end the Coast Guard always asks, "Are you and your vessel in any immediate danger?"

I held back the urge to yell, "What do you think, you Southern grit, it's blowing a million, I'm dead in the water, and I'm dodging flying log books, coffee pots, and anything else that's not nailed down."

Instead, I tell them nicely, "No, just send someone to come get us. Please."

An hour or so goes by before I'm informed that the 300-foot Coast Guard cutter in Kodiak can't make it out of Women's Bay because it's blowing too hard and the Coast Guard would try to send a boat from Seward.

By the next morning we had drifted about thirty miles closer to Kodiak. The boat from Seward never did make it away from the dock, but the large cutter in Kodiak was now en route. The wind had died to a mere screaming gale of around 45 knots and the seas were running about 12-footers.

The *Prosperity* was totally trashed and the crew was a mixture of angry, tired, and scared. I found myself all alone in the wheelhouse because no one would come within eyesight of me. I think the whole crew thought maybe I'd be okay if they just gave me a little quiet time.

The cutter would be on the scene in about five hours and I would finally have a tow. Meanwhile, our office didn't know the cutter was en route and had hired a commercial tug to get us. By law, the Coast Guard can't tow a vessel if commercial assistance has been hired. The estimated time of arrival of the commercial tug was twelve hours and they thought they could tow us at about 3 or 4 knots once they hooked up. The cutter, on the other hand, would have probably made about 10 knots and could have had me alongside a dock by the time the tug even arrived on the scene. I went into another rage as I read the telex from Seattle and realized I'd have to drift for another twelve hours.

At 2 a.m. the following morning the so-called tug, which turned out to be a mud boat with very little horsepower, arrived. Mud boats are old supply boats that were brought up from the Gulf of Mexico, where they were used in the oil industry. The boat attached us to their hawser and began the slow tow towards Kodiak. Meanwhile, the great big gas turbine Coast Guard cutter escorted us in.

After seventy-two hours from the time I lost my power, I was finally alongside the dock. I hadn't slept and probably looked like an escaped, crazed mental patient. The Coast Guard boarding team just looked at me and said, "We'll come back in the morning. We just have a few questions and some paperwork. It can wait."

A scuba diver arrived the following morning, along with the Coast Guard to take my statements. After a few, "I'm sorry, hope things work out, good luck, see yas," they were gone. The diver reported after thirty seconds in the water that we had a large codend in both nozzles wrapped around the shafts and tucked in around the rudders.

"The good news is there are no cables or chain, it's just web," he said.

"Great," I said quietly, "thanks, that sure brightens up my morning."

The diver figured he could have the net out in six to eight hours and back underwater he went.

Thankfully, the rest of the spring season was better and we put in some good trips. By mid-May I was more than ready to go join Barb in Washington.

A CHILD IS BORN

Barb was now over six months along in her pregnancy. After completing her shore plant observing contract in Dutch Harbor in March, she had returned to South Bend, Washington. She kept busy by finishing up the remodeling a small duplex she had purchased the year before when she had moved to the area to do spotted owl surveys. We were going to move her and all her belongings to my home in Alaska, and she decided to put the duplex on the market to sell.

We figured I'd better get off the boat and start this journey before the baby was too far along. I had visions of delivering my child somewhere deep in British Columbia on some deserted stretch of the Alcan Highway. I had to get off the boat.

Barb had this old Toyota pickup she insisted was a good truck and that it would make the trip towing a trailer with her belongings. I kept telling her no way and urged her to buy a good four-wheel drive rig, but she insisted she liked her truck and it would make it to Alaska just fine.

She picked me up with her parents in Seattle, looking nothing like being six months pregnant. She appeared strong and thin, with just a little beer belly, and she looked extremely healthy. I, on the other hand, looked terrible after five months of fishing. I even had a partial mohawk that I had joined the crew in doing during one of our lapses of sanity towards the end.

After many hugs and kisses we made our way to the parking garage and Barb goes right up to a Jeep Cherokee. I signal her to get away from that rig and, by the way, where is her old truck?

Surprise. I'm on the receiving end of a family joke. But at least I wouldn't have to drive 2,000 miles in an old pickup.

Her step-dad, Harold, and I built a utility trailer from an old house trailer frame in about three days at her folks' home in Olympia, with the help of one of their neighbors. We packed her up and carefully loaded the trailer to the top.

It was way overloaded and Harold said, "No way, you two won't make it as far as Seattle towing that thing."

We ended up putting about a third of the load in that old Toyota pickup, which had a canopy. She was right. That pickup did make it to Alaska and I drove it almost the entire way since she was more comfortable in the Jeep.

The trip north took us over two weeks. Some days we drove only fifty miles, and others we covered over 300. We had a great time camping along the way, taking time for me to ski in Whistler, British Columbia, and in general enjoying the drive, scenery, and each other's company on this remote highway that takes you into the far reaches of Canada before entering Alaska.

We arrived in Girdwood on June 1, 1995, and started to turn my cedar resort house into the beginning of a beautiful bed and breakfast. We also picked lots of wild berries that we made into over fifty pints of freezer jam, and caught and smoked lots of salmon. Anything to help pass the time during Barb's last stage of pregnancy. At last our daughter, Dancia, was born on August 7. I was a father and extremely happy. Fishing and the ocean was, for the first time in my life, the farthest thing from my mind. I took the rest of the year off.

NOT NECESSARILY PROSPERITY

The year 1996 would be my final year on *Prosperity*. It was a good year and the vessel grossed over four million dollars—the most ever in its sad history. Somehow, however, the company wasn't paying the bills and the crew was perpetually late in receiving their checks.

The year ended in early November with a blown main engine. We were on a cash-only basis with most of the shoreside support companies in Dutch Harbor and limped back to Seattle on one engine, making a slow 6 knots of speed all the way across the Gulf of Alaska. The office had a lot to answer for.

We were told that the checks were not ready. The excuse was that the company was sitting on large inventories of product and also awaiting checks themselves on the fish that had already been sold. The crew and I needed the money. We felt disheartened and discouraged that we weren't getting paid as quickly as promised.

Most of the crew, including myself, found jobs on other boats with different companies. Our trust in ScanSea, Ltd., was broken. Eight months later, I found myself still waiting for all of my wages from *Prosperity*. I eventually was paid, but only after a great deal of persistence on my part. It wasn't right.

One memorable event during my final year aboard *Prosperity* occurred during our second roe trip of *A* season in February. My foreman, Emerson, an ex-military gun nut, drill sergeant-type guy, reported to me that we had a Section 8 case.

"What the hell is a Section 8?" I asked.

"Nut case," Emerson said.

Now in the past I've had a crewmember that thought he saw Wolf Blitzer in a skiff, and another who just couldn't stop crying, but these guys weren't really crazy, just tired or something. The guy Emerson was talking about was nuts. Really bonkers. I'll call him Animal, for that's what he looked like. When I saw him, his eyes were bugged out and he was shaking kind of bad.

Animal was convinced the whole gang was going to kill him and the only guy he'd talk to was a Rasta deckhand named Ed. I guess he thought Ed understood him. Animal wouldn't sleep and was now on his third straight day of being awake. When Emerson finally told me about him, he was in a corner of the factory talking aloud to his mom, who was thousands of miles away.

Emerson told me our engineer, Koob, was in the workshop making up a pair of shackles. Koob wanted the guy in irons, since he was starting to freak out some of the crew. I found it amazing that the captain is the last to find out about some things, and this was one of them.

We had a situation on our hands. First, I talked Koob out of chaining the guy to a piece of machinery. Then I went to see the guy, who didn't trust me in the least. We ended up putting him in confinement in a four-man stateroom and Ed, the Rasta, was placed on 24-hour watch duty.

We were just about full of fish, so I finished the trip while keeping in close contact with a doctor in Seattle via our costly satellite telephone system. The doctor told me to medicate him, but Animal thought I was trying to poison him and refused a sedative. Meanwhile, Ed just kept on talking to him, trying to keep him somewhat calm.

The Coast Guard, police, and medics were waiting for us when we arrived in Dutch Harbor. I pulled the boat up to a fuel dock and was sitting in my chair in the wheelhouse when they all came rushing in. It was about 15°F outside and snowing, but in the wheelhouse it was 75°F and I just so happened to be in shorts and wearing my moose booties.

"Is that the guy?" the rescue crew asked, pointing at me.

I'll never forget Emerson clearing his throat calmly before telling them, "No, that's not him, he's our captain. The medical is down in the galley with the Rasta."

The rescue crew probably thought about half of us should be admitted.

THE REBECCA IRENE

After *Prosperity*, my new job involved returning to Golden Age Fisheries, the company that had owned the *Golden Fleece*. I met back up with Bill Sage, their operations manager, in December 1996. The captain position on their factory trawler the *Rebecca Irene* was available. I assured him I could catch the fish he needed, an agreement came easily, and I had a new boat with my old company.

The *Rebecca Irene* is a vessel that I'd admired for years. It was built in 1987 in the heyday of bottomfishing in Alaska. In today's markets and given the current state of the fishing industry, a boat like the *Rebecca Irene* would be too costly to build. The boat is 150 feet overall in length, draws over 20 feet of water, and can pack over 280 metric tons of finished frozen fish product. It has almost 2,000 horsepower, holds a crew of thirty-eight people, and is one of the best trawlers ever built for its size.

From my old crew I managed to bring a couple of people, including Lilly Beauchamp, my cook for seven years, and Upia, my Samoan deckhand. The vessel came with good core personnel, some of who had been with the boat for many years.

Our *A* season of fishing in January 1997 was very good and turned out to be my personal best. We produced over 500 metric tons of rock sole roe fish and over 1,000 tons of total product. It was one of the vessel's better roe seasons in the last few years.

After taking off a few weeks in late spring, I returned to work a rewarding summer *B* season. It began in July and targeted flathead sole, with deepwater bycatch that included turbot, black cod, and thorny head rockfish.

It was a short season, but still I missed getting home for Dancia's second birthday on August 7, and my thirty-fifth birthday on August 9. Since I had been gone Dancia had grown and changed into a different little girl. Into the eighth month of the year, I had been gone to sea all but six weeks and was ready for a long break.

Whenever I returned home from being at sea, Barb and I would take some quiet time with Dancia for about a week before we went out in public. We'd post a note on our front door that basically told people to leave us alone nicely. The days when I first get back are my most special days. They are lazy and we fill the hours with drinking champagne, sleeping in until whenever, enjoying the hot tub on our back deck, and playing long hours with Dancia. Then we'd start to get that Alaskan itch that drew us outside.

Summer and fall in Girdwood for the three of us was filled with adventure. We'd mountain bike along the Resurrection Pass with Dancia riding behind Barb in a child seat, float the Kenai River in our drift boat, hike mountain trails, and explore the state. This would take us right into hunting season, which Barb and I still hadn't quite worked out. She didn't put quite the priority I did on the many trips I planned, although she loves to eat the meat it brings.

By the first of September our black labs would let me know when duck hunting season was upon us. They were always eager and insisted on it, so I would end up going along. At times they can be very persistent. Then moose season came along, goat areas opened up, and before I knew it, sheep season would only have a mere twenty days left. To add to the congestion, fishing for rainbows and Dolly Vardens is best in September.

With so much to fill my time, for some crazy reason I decided to start building a deck, a big deck, out in front of our home on August 29. I'm no builder and I must have thought that a deck just appears after a few nails get pounded. I hired a local named Twirl and we took on the project together. Barb agreed to this after I made the deal I'd see it through to the end.

"Sure, you betcha, a deck—no problem. I'll even help build it," I told her, and then called up Harold and asked him to come help, enticing him with a hunting trip afterwards and a free plane ticket from Washington. I was sure we'd have it built in no time.

We were getting well into the project after the first two days when it started to rain, and it rained hard. This slowed the project considerably and in the end it turned out a lot of September days were spent pounding nails. I learned a very important lesson to never, ever start a major project in late August in Alaska.

At the end of October the office wanted me to mop up the remainder of the fishing season. I pleaded to be excused from November's Bering Sea hell month and Bill Sage came through. The remainder of the year was mostly mine.

On December 1, I flew to Seattle to go over shipyard lists and discuss with the owner of the company a new $500,000 factory he planned on putting in the *Rebecca Irene*. I returned to Alaska feeling extremely excited about the coming year.

Two days later I received a call from Bill Sage telling me Christiana Bank, a Norwegian bank that held the notes on the company's two boats, had just put the hammer down and foreclosed on the company. Both boats had U.S. Marshal stickers placed on them at the docks. Bam. Just like that I go from having a $130,000-a-year job to being unemployed and collecting unemployment.

This whole thing came to be because the state of Alaska stepped in and forced a split with Golden Age Fisheries and the Alaska Native corporation they were partners with for their second vessel, the *Brown's Point*. In the process, Golden Age lost the Community Development Quota program that was the *Brown's Point* future. The *Rebecca Irene* just so happened to be caught in that avalanche and went down also, even though it had been a big money maker for the company.

I was devastated. The boat I'd waited for since I first saw her in 1988 in Kodiak was out of service. I felt like the way most must feel when you lose your job. Barb helped to bring me back into focus like only she can, and I started to feel better.

"We'll buckle down and not spend any money—not even on coffee to go at the 7-11. We have our season passes for skiing paid for and we'll ski," she said. Strangely, all my old ski buddies didn't seem to feel sorry for me. They didn't understand the work side of my life when I wasn't playing hard in Girdwood.

As the reality of the situation set in, the big picture first started to come into focus. As in so many things, you need to step away from something to really see it in its entirety. The commercial fishing for groundfish was slowly becoming a dying industry and would be a different fishery in the near future. It was already different from when I first started with the factory boats not that many years before.

I found myself feeling very sad. I loved how I made my living and missed the friendships of my crew and the other captains and mates I'd talk for hours with on the marine radio while at sea. I missed so much and wondered if I would ever get it back.

With my heart and soul, I wanted it back, but at the same time began to think perhaps it was time to turn away. I'd been successful and seen the best of many fisheries. It would be kind of like a quarterback retiring when he's still in his peak. Still, I had too many good games in me yet to be played. I wasn't going to give up. There had to be a way to get it all back.

COMPANY HOPPING FOR THE REBECCA IRENE

The *Rebecca Irene* sat un-owned for less than six months during 1998, tied to a federal marshal repossession dock in Ballard. I kept track of potential buyers and kept in contact with three different companies that looked the most promising. The boat was too good of deal to sit for long, and I wanted to be hired by whichever new company pulled a deal together. I kept in contact with my key personnel, who I considered to be an extended family. We were all in the same boat, with employment opportunities dwindling in our field.

Iquique U.S., LLC, a company that managed four other trawlers that fished Alaskan waters, managed to put together the best offer when the *Rebecca Irene* was sold on the block. They purchased the boat for around $3 million, which was a steal. The boat was easily worth $6–7 million. My diligence paid off, and they hired me and a large percentage of my former crew back to operate the vessel. We were back in business, and it was a win-win situation for all.

The previous six months of waiting was quickly fading to the hazy part of my memory. When I look back, I realize it was the best time of my marriage. Barb and I skied every day, were able to do the Friday night ski racing series at Alyeska together, spent wonderful quality time with Dancia, had great home cooked meals shared with friends, and lived off the income from Girdwood Escape Bed and Breakfast that Barb had turned into a successful small business out of our home. True to our word, we didn't spend much money. When my folks sent us $50 to go out to a nice dinner, we bought a case of Cooks champagne instead. Not once did we have to dip into our savings.

Removed from the temptations of being at sea, which too often involved other women, I was a good husband for one of the few times in our marriage. I should have quit fishing then. Perhaps I would still be married to Barb. Regardless, I would not have gotten into the trouble I was heading towards that would eventually end my fishing career.

In June 1998 as I returned to work, the normal jitters of starting with a new company didn't exist for me. I was too excited. I spent a month working on the boat at the Seattle shipyard and helping the Iquique office get the boat out of mothballs. I was cocky and roaring to go.

This second wind created a super-competitive streak in me. It was also the stretch in my career where everything began to catch up with me. For the next 3-1/2 years I took the company and industry by storm. We were the top boat in the company and I'd be surprised to learn that anyone in the groundfish fleet fishing the Bering Sea did as good during the span from 1998 to 2000. The company was happy and even made me a small percentage partner in the boat in 1999. I felt like I was riding on top of the fishing world.

A Tribute to Hook

During the past ten years fishing near Unimak Pass in the Bering Sea, I'd become friendly with a large group of killer whales. As with the other boats I'd been on, the huge mammals always seemed to be waiting to welcome the *Rebecca Irene* when our search for bottomfish takes us to the pass. And readier, still, for the feast of fish heads dished out through the discard chute of the trawler.

I'd gotten to know individual whales in the Unimak pod well enough to name them. The group is led by a huge, dominant male we called Bent Fin for his massive six-foot dorsal fin that has a couple of funny tweaks in it. Other prominent members included a female with two babies in tow and a piece of her fin missing we called Chunk; Bumps, a playful calf covered in lumps; Goofy, who seemed to spend more time swimming upside down than right side up; and old Hook, the largest of them all with his dorsal fin laid across his back and too elderly to challenge Bent Fin for leadership of the pod.

If I were a longline fisherman, I'd almost certainly not have such a friendly relationship with these whales. Orcas (killer whales) learn to eat sablefish and turbot right off the longliners' hooks, and such vessels can lose an entire catch to the thieves. Since the *Rebecca Irene* is a factory trawler, the orcas don't bite through the meshes of net or codend that we tow behind us. Instead, they seem content to dine on the leftovers from our onboard processing plant.

The floor of the Bering Sea is like an undersea plain that gradually rises into shallows near Bristol Bay. Just north of Unimak Pass is an area called the horseshoe, which lies on the eastern edge of the deep water. The horseshoe is a very productive fishing ground and is also the summer home of the Unimak pod.

The *Rebecca Irene* would frequently trawl for groundfish there, harvesting various species of sole, flounder, Pacific cod, sablefish, and turbot. The orcas that followed us became picky eaters. Turbot heads were their clear favorites with sablefish (also called black cod) running a close second. The whales would actually spit out a perfectly good arrowtooth flounder head if they spotted a turbot snack within easy reach.

Before the whales could eat, our net must be brought onboard and the codend dumped, sending the catch below deck for processing. Between haulbacks when the factory runs out of fish to process, the flow of whale treats out the discard chute stops. The Unimak pod would respond immediately to this outrage. This would usually take form in about ten minutes of tail slapping with each one cracking like a rifle shot, and spy-hopping, which involves raising the front halves of their bodies from the water to look on the deck or peer at me in the wheelhouse. They honestly seemed to be trying to figure out what the hold-up was.

If the discard chutes still didn't spit out any fish following this display, the whales would pull away about a hundred yards or more and lazily keep pace with the boat. As soon as they heard the hydraulics kick in to raise the net, the whole pod would come charging back and the tail slapping and spy-hopping would begin again. Goofy would commence swimming in circles upside down, and old Hook would take up his traditional position at the back of the boat, patiently waiting for lunch.

When I returned to the fishing grounds in April of 1998, the Unimak pod was already there, as usual, having arrived at the horseshoe from wherever it is they spend their winters. I stood at the rail and waved to the ones I recognized, feeling only a little foolish. Old Goofy came close to the boat, spy-hopping so high that only her tail remained in the water, and seemed to look me right in the eye. She repeated this greeting five times before backing off and returning to the peaceful monotony of her upside-down patrols.

All was not well, however. After I'd been in the pod's territory for more than a week, I had yet to see old Hook. Each day new members of the extended orca family turned up, but the ancient patriarch didn't show. Since he's the largest of seven or eight mature males that are the pod's big bucks, I knew he was well into orca senior citizen status. Maybe, I speculated, the long trip to the summer grounds was too much for him this year. Perhaps he decided to hang out in Southeast Alaska and entertain the cruise ships. Or had he gone on to that great fishing ground in the sky?

Each morning with my first cup of coffee in hand, I'd go to the rail to greet the pod and welcome new arrivals. "Still no Hook," I'd mumble to myself before heading back to the wheelhouse, worry nagging me. But then, on April 26, as I greeted a beautiful morning and a light southeast wind with a latte in hand, I stepped outside just in time to see Hook glide by the ship's starboard side.

"Hello, old fellow," I said grinning despite of myself, "glad you've finally arrived." I lifted my mug in a toast, and Hook rolled on his side in seeming acknowledgement, with huge brown eyes looking into mine.

Hook was clearly hungry. He took up a rightful prime feeding spot at the bottom of the discard chute. The other whales seemed to back off, as if consciously giving him, for this day at least, first choice of the groceries. He looked a bit thin, as if suffering the effects of old age and a long, difficult swim from somewhere. But for the moment, at least, he was done with hardship.

"Your worries are over, old boy," I said really to myself, "it's haulback time."

THE WAY OF THE WIND

I have never had a bit of interest in sailing and not in a million years could I ever envision myself owning a sailboat, let alone living on one. My home in Girdwood was a massive cedar home two miles from the ski slopes and was a lifelong dream home. I thought I'd grow old in this house. But when I married Barb in 1995, I made the promise to her, probably in bed, that I'd follow her dream of cruising the world's oceans.

We had talked about our plans often with each other, and once in a while with everyone else. No one seemed to take us seriously, and we'd often receive blank stares or empty "oh, that's nice" responses, especially after our second child, a son we named Jamie, arrived in March of 1999. The few that enthusiastically encouraged us would buy us Christmas and birthday gifts related to cruising—almost daring us to do it.

By May of 1999, we began checking out boat dealers in Southern California while on a vacation to Disneyland. It was rather comical meeting to look at boats with a three-month-old baby in a front sling on Barb, with an energetic three-year-old with eager eyes tagging along. To their credit, the few brokers we met treated us well. They assured us they'd keep in touch and would keep us posted about boats that may fit what we were looking for. We never heard from any of them again. I imagine we became more than one topic of happy hour conversations in the boat broker world. I think they'd all be in shock to learn we bought a boat within a month.

One broker we met with was very kind. He showed us a boat I liked a lot, and another one Barb liked better. He sensed our differences, which were really small things in terms of picking a long-term cruising vessel. He told us when we found the right boat, we'd know it. He was right.

In June of 1999 during a stopover in Seattle we bought the Jack of Hearts, a 44-foot Lancer motorsailer. The boat had a comfortable, family-friendly design that sailed well but also had the sailing version of an inside wheelhouse. It was time to make our pact to be sailing by the year 2000 a reality.

By September, I found myself loaded up with the kids and our black lab towing a trailer yet again on the Alcan Highway. My stomach was in knots with my life in Alaska behind me, as I was about to take on a journey that would change my life forever.

Living onboard a sailboat so small that I could put it on the back deck of the Rebecca Irene, with two kids and a dog, was an enormous culture shock for me. I was not a nice guy to be around. My attitude was poor at best too much of the time, and I took out my emotions on my wife and the dog the most. This was really the beginning of the end of my marriage, as one person's dream was fast becoming another's nightmare.

I drove the boat through the Ballard locks and Barb became in charge of all the skippering after that. We spent the first nine months shaking down the boat while living at Semiahmoo Marina in Blaine, Washington. It is located fifteen miles from the San Juan Islands, which we explored at every chance. We even hired a teenage nanny for the summer of 2000 so that Barb could continue to use the boat in the San Juans while I was out fishing.

While I fished the summer *B* season on the *Rebecca Irene*, Barb took the boat down the Pacific Coast in August with three girlfriends while her mom watched the kids. She wanted to be sure the boat was seaworthy before taking the children along. When I rejoined Barb and the kids, we spent a month at a San Diego marina spending a boatload of money outfitting the boat for offshore cruising with electronics, an autopilot, generator, watermaker, and supplies. Soon the boat was ready to head offshore.

We had originally planned to sail to Mexico before embarking on the Coconut Milk Run to Fiji. However, while in San Diego we heard about a new marina, Ko Olina, on the island of Oahu. It sounded spectacular and was offering liveaboard slips at half the cost of marinas we had checked out in Mexico. We decided to head there instead and by early November of 2000 we set sail across the vast Pacific to the Hawaiian Islands. This twenty-day ocean crossing was one I'll never forget and I actually found myself enjoying the journey. I got to fish from sunrise to sunset and became extremely close to my two children.

Arriving in the islands I quickly bonded with the fishermen and a new focus quickly filled the void of Alaska. Marlin fishing became my new addiction and the problem of owning a sailboat instead of sport fishing boat had to be overcome. I had a few things going for me. The *Jack of Hearts* had a back deck like a back porch and I transformed her into a game boat. As I started to figure out the billfish and I began catching a lot of them on a very nontraditional boat, I found myself having a ball.

During 2001 and 2002, we explored all the Hawaiian Islands during every school break for Dancia and my off time from fishing in Alaska. I was still making pretty big money and we could afford to use the boat in a pretty decadent way exploring ports along the entire chain of islands, from Kona, on the Big Island, to Kauai. We found spectacular anchorages with snorkeling and kayaking, and of course there was pelagic fishing all along the way. Barb and I had our share of disagreements over her wanting to put up the sails and me running the engine hard enough to get our speed up fast enough to pulling lure speed. I won 99 percent of these battles, as she liked to eat the fish too. She became a pretty good angler and caught her share of tuna, wahoo, and billfish, but her idea of enjoying a nice sail drove me batshit. I knew I'd never become a true sailor.

BACK TO FISHING

Like always with me, I'll stir up a nest of hornets just for the hell of it. When I get comfortable and settled in, regardless of what it is in my life, the rebel comes out. I would have made a great pirate.

I started to question a lot of what I was seeing in the company operations for the *Rebecca Irene*. I disagreed with the huge Danish influence that seemed to dominate management decisions, and I openly let my opinions be known in the office, which in turn stirred up fires.

Initially, I had worked alongside one of Iquique's Danish captains on the *Cape Horn*, a 165-foot factory trawler. He learned my secret areas and the allowable bycatch game from me, but I soon realized the sharing of knowledge was a one-way street. Taking nothing away from the guy, for he is a good fisherman, I began to realize his higher stocks and success were coming from the areas and a fishing style that I brought to the company. It was a lopsided situation and I rebelled. It was the start of my troubles with the company.

The year 2001 was an off year. Water temperatures in January and February were what they usually are in July in the Bering Sea. The *A* fishing season was off for the whole groundfish fleet, and our company was down about 20 percent from the past averages.

Spring shutdown occurs from mid-May to early July, when the fish are all spawned out and hold low market value. It's a time when most boats travel back to shipyards for maintenance and repairs. What followed for the *Rebecca Irene* was a series of piss poor management decisions led by the Danish influence that thought they knew best, and left me getting pissed off and turning into Blackbeard reincarnate.

My marriage was on the rocks. Barb, being a very smart woman, knew what was going on onboard the boat regarding other women and she had had enough of the lies, cheating, and bullshit. My anger problem was escalating at home and onboard. Now the Danish element was telling me how to run my boat and the God damn El Nino was messing with my ocean. All this just pissed me off.

That summer before the July start-up of the lucrative *B* season, I was told a new factory foreman was being brought onboard. Our old foreman was a crackerjack who had been with the boat since the Golden Age ownership days, but the Danish wanted this new guy instead. The new guy was of Norwegian descent and had worked on pollock boats, which has a different factory setup and is a whole different ballgame in terms of running the factory. It didn't sound good.

I was livid about having never been asked about this management decision that affected an extremely important crew position. I tried calling and meeting with the company president numerous times to try and turn this around, but was told the decision wasn't mine to make.

As I predicted, production dropped a lot. The fish came up the ramp as normal, but just couldn't make it through the factory as fast. The office barked and I barked back. Tensions built and the low production numbers kept getting thrown in my face. I knew that if I couldn't get the volume through the factory, I'd have to try and put more high value fish onboard. With fish prices in the toilet, it was a struggle at best. The whole crew was under a massive strain.

The new guy lasted four months, but it was an entire year before I could finally convince the company to bring my old foreman back.

TROUBLE BEGINS

Foss Shipyard, Seattle, December 2001

"Cork, I got a call from a federal marshal," Big Frank said with a worried expression, as he tentatively handed me a latte in the galley.

"Huh? When? What the hell did he want? You shitting me?" I said, struggling to hold back a scream resonating from the depths of my stomach. "Frank, I'm not in the mood for this."

Frank began to look really anxious and unsure.

"I'll be right back," I said, leaping two flights up to the wheelhouse of the *Rebecca Irene*.

I looked out the side windows to make sure the cops, FBI, ATF, and maybe even the CIA, weren't storming over the rails of the boat. The coast was clear. It looked safe for now.

"Frank!" I yelled down, summoning the 300-pound monster of a Samoan to join me.

In a soft voice you would never match to the man, he said, "Yeah, Cork, he asked a lot of questions about us pre-sorting halibut."

Oh man. I ran to the side door and out to the bow, where I bent over the rails to look at the name of the boat. *Rebecca Irene* in huge white letters. Yeap, the right boat. I tore my wallet out of my pocket and began to fumble with it. A gust of wind scattered its contents on the deck. Staring up at me was my Alaska state driver's license. Mark S. Decker. Okay, that's me. I ran back to the wheelhouse, gasping for breath.

"You okay, Captain?" Frank asked, looking more than a little worried.

"No. Yes. I don't know! Okay, tell me everything."

Twenty minutes later I made a call to our office. I told the company president what Frank had told me and fully expected to be ordered to bring Frank and myself to the office NOW to get debriefed. Instead, I was greeted by silence on the other end.

"Uh, did you hear me? We're under investigation by the Feds," I once again informed him in a shaky voice.

"How's the new factory coming?" he asked in response.

"I gotta go," I said, slamming down the cell phone on the chart table. He doesn't believe me, was all I could think.

This should have been a big red flag of things to come, but instead I put the matter into storage in the clouded regions of my mind and went back to work. Perhaps I was over reacting, I convinced myself.

We were installing a brand new stainless steel factory on the *Rebecca Irene* and the cost for the factory alone was upwards of a million dollars. We were also putting in a new winch drive system on the trawl deck and doing a total rebuild of the main engine and two generators. This sent shipyard bills to $1.3 million and the costs were still climbing. All this was on the tail end of an off year where our boat gross went from $6.7 million down to $5.8 million. The pressure was on.

Pressure? Yeah, I thrive in pressure situations. As a fisherman, I love it. The competition, the drive, the money, is all fueled by the people who depend on my success as a captain. At the time this included over thirty crewmembers and their families, office personnel, and support businesses such as fuel docks, airlines, coastal transports, runners, and logistic personnel. Our combined effort yielded an annual product that fed literally millions of people, not to mention making each of us a good living.

To meet these expectations, a few rules get bent. In plain black and white, laws are broken. My whole life I'd learned with teachers, parents, relationships, etc., that dishonesty can be an easy out. But never have I learned it more so than in this business, where owners and management make it plainly known that you're only as good as your last trip. If you make $6 million one year, you better make $6.5 million the next. Profits and the bottom line is all that matters to these people.

In the words of one owner, "I don't care how you do it. Get those numbers up."

Fish prices had been dropping everywhere and we were getting paid about one quarter less per pound than we did ten years before. Meanwhile, fuel prices had nearly doubled, insurance escalated, and other costs such as shipping, airfares, nets, doors, twine, and materials continued to go up. The only solution was to catch more fish. Always. More fish up the ramp means more fish through the factory. It's all about money.

On the other side of the dollar bill is the environmental factor and the whole absurd bycatch issue itself. We were throwing back millions of pounds of valuable and desirable seafood. By *law*, we must throw back all prohibited species, dead or alive, and even our target species if we reach a certain cap. The allowable catch of halibut or sometimes crab, both prohibited species, is usually what we eat up first.

Other countries don't have this problem. Bycatch isn't even an issue, for they keep and sell most of everything they catch. That's the saddest part of the fisheries management system in Alaska and elsewhere in the United States. Our practices are dictated and enforced by NMFS. There are laws we must abide by, unless we find illegal ways around them. Our fish stocks are constantly monitored and managed, we have increased competition from other boats, and still we must be able to pull in the gross stocks demanded of us at sea to make a profit. With all the starving people in the world, being forced to throw over these fish seems more than asinine to me. It is immoral, wrong, and something that has bothered me throughout my career.

Overwhelming? Odds stacked against us? Impossible? Nah, we've had years to fine-tune the game. We're good at it and we prove this year in and year out, with high boat grosses, high wages, and massive padded pockets of the higher ups.

Until, that is, we get caught.

GETTING CAUGHT

A disgruntled assistant engineer was fired in the late summer of 2001 for stealing narcotics from the ship's medical chest. I had no choice but to fire him on the spot and have him sent home at the next offload. He had been with the boat through ownership changes and had become part of the extended family onboard. The news that he was leaving shocked the crew. A former felon, his new direction in life and career had now been ruined by his own actions. He was back at ground zero.

He stewed on his own demise for three months before calling the NMFS enforcement office in Dutch Harbor. He reported that the boat routinely pre-sorted halibut and that I ordered it, a serious offense. He was lashing back and saw me as his demise, even though I had been dedicated to encouraging him to reach for becoming a licensed engineer.

That, in very simple and broad terms, explains how I as the captain of a 150-foot factory trawler got caught breaking the law. I did it. I'm guilty. Without trying to make excuses, I will explain how the pre-sorting of a groundfish whose population has exploded in all of our Alaskan waters can lead to the demise of a career fisherman.

Prohibited species is the term NMFS likes to call species that include halibut, salmon, herring, king crab, and tanner crabs. They're protected in much the same way as threatened or endangered marine mammals and sea birds are. Whenever they are caught they must be returned to the ocean, dead or alive. But first a fisheries observer for NMFS, who lives and works onboard, must have the opportunity to collect data and count them in their tallies and samples. Otherwise, their true numbers won't be known. Observers are basically the NMFS version of a fish cop.

A NMFS fisheries observer is required at all times on vessels over 125 feet, while vessels between 65 and 125 feet are only required to have an observer onboard 30 percent of the time they fish. Vessels smaller than 65 feet usually don't fish the waters we fish, but when they do, they have the ultimate advantage, as they aren't required to take an observer at all.

An observer's job is to collect data. They monitor and estimate the size of the catch brought onboard vessels, record the fishing location and depth, and conduct samples on the fish caught. They wear many hats, including recording marine mammal and seabird observations, and often conduct special research projects in addition to their daily monitoring of the fishery. Information obtained by observers is sent to NMFS fisheries management and aids them in making an independent determination of the the total catch brought onboard, whether processed or discarded. The data is used by NMFS to monitor fish populations, set catch limits, and monitor interactions with protected seabirds and marine mammals.

Observers are hired by private companies that contract their work out to the fishing companies to meet the NMFS requirements for coverage. NMFS provides the certification and training for each individual that is sent out on a boat, and each vessel pays a fee to have them onboard that covers their salaries, expenses, and their management company's fees. They have free range onboard and are considered independent from the company, even though they live and work alongside the rest of us. They can basically show up wherever they want, whenever they want. Their job of collecting data is made extremely difficult by the games we play to bias their data, no matter how much we like them as people.

How observers estimate the total size of the catch has become a fairly sophisticated undertaking which often involves measurements on deck before the fish can be processed. The boat also keeps its own estimate of the size of the catch to report to NMFS, which is usually determined by the skipper eyeballing the fish brought onboard and making an estimate. This estimate is based on days in and days out of seeing nets brought onboard and knowing the tonnage of fish that are eventually processed. If the skipper's estimate is honest and the observer knows what they're doing, the two estimates are usually close.

Depending on the fishery and the purity of the catch, the observers will either "whole haul" the entire catch and pull out every prohibited species caught, or conduct basket samples that make up a sub-sample of the catch. Only very pure fisheries such as midwater trawling for pollock allow the observer to conduct whole haul samples. For the most part in the groundfish industry, basket samples are the norm for observers.

The observers follow a random sample table that tells them which haul they're required to sample. In-between samples they figure out the best time to sleep, and often exist on a rotating schedule around the clock where they catch pockets of sleep whenever they can. Ideally their data collection consists of different samples of fish taken from the beginning, middle, and end of each net full of fish, called a tow. Since the stronger fish such as halibut often swim forward in the nets, this is the only way to get an accurate picture of the total catch.

For basket samples, they identify all the species caught in their sample, record their numbers and weights, and list it all on a data sheet. These figures are sent electronically to NMFS and the data is extrapolated. It provides an estimation of the total species composition for that particular tow.

Pre-sorting, in simple terms, is biasing the observer's data. As fishermen we are only allowed X amount of each prohibited species.

Once these caps are reached, we are shut down, regardless of whether we reached our allowable quota of the target species such as cod, rock sole, etc. Getting shut down because of reaching the limits of prohibited species happens 99 percent of the time. The longer we can stretch out the prohibited species cap, the longer we fish and the more money we all make.

Learning how to bias the observer's basket samples has become a fine art. We all do it, to one extent or another. Some of the boats are masters of the game, while others are very subtle, but from my experience it is done fleet-wide.

For the groundfish fleet we generally have one observer onboard, although some of the larger pollock boats have two. Halibut is the most common prohibited species we catch, since they occur everywhere in Alaskan waters in prolific numbers. To remove a fair number of halibut without the observer knowing any better is simple. The observer can only be one place at one time, and we just throw them overboard when the observer isn't present.

This gives us two options. Watching a codend being dumped from the deck into a live tank for a 20-ton tow can take five minutes or more for the observer. As the observer watches from the deck, the crew can run a lot of halibut overboard through the discard chute in the factory. When the observer goes below into the factory to their sampling station, any remaining halibut out of the observer's sight from below gets chucked overboard from the deck level. Usually this is done by the deck crew removing the fish from the live tank via the hatch on deck that the tow was dumped into, as long as the observer can't see.

There are many other methods I've personally used or I've heard of other boats using, but this book would make a Tom Clancy novel seem like a magazine if I went into them all. Let's just say over the years commercial fishermen have learned so many ways to work around the existing system that it makes it close to impossible for the observer program to get good honest data.

Boats required to have only 30 percent observer coverage have it even easier. This ruling basically gives them a license to steal. The data collected during their observer coverage period is used to project a fleet-wide average that is grossly inaccurate.

When I ran a 30 percent boat in the early 1990s, for 70 percent of the time fishing clean and avoiding areas where large numbers of prohibited bycatch were present rarely entered the picture. During these unobserved periods, boats would have a total free-for-all.

Even the smallest boats (under 65 feet) hold a significant amount of product. These boats include 56-foot seiners that are rigged up for trawling and deliver their fish to shoreside plants. They can pack over 200,000 pounds of cod into their tanks. Since they're less than 65 feet, they're not required to take a fisheries observer at any time. They basically have a license to have a field day.

Some factory trawlers are under 125 feet long, but they are deep draft vessels with crews of up to thirty people. These boats process over 25 metric tons of frozen product a day and hold over 250 metric tons of product in their holds. They are not small vessels.

My best guess is at least 100 percent more than the total prohibited species quota allowed as bycatch to be discarded are not reported by these boats. Add on what the big boats hide, and the current fisheries management system is seriously flawed. It's a perfect example of laws that don't apply to everyone, but should, and it is a broken system, at best.

The NMFS enforcement office in Dutch Harbor is a place no Alaskan fisherman in his right mind would walk into asking, "What's up? You people investigating me?" But that's just what I did in April of 2002.

BUSTED

By spring of 2002, my NMFS observers were letting me know that they were being drilled by NMFS enforcement in Dutch Harbor every time we were in town. After three months, I couldn't take it anymore and went into the lion's den.

Ernie Soper, a balding and friendly fish cop, was the head of the NMFS investigation that was building against me. He told me in plain English that yes, I was under an intense investigation for presorting halibut. He even went so far as to show me a desk drawer full of documents.

I felt like I had just got sacked by Junior Seau. My lungs couldn't get any air and I started to shake uncontrollably. My whole damn life had just changed, yet still at that time I didn't know the full scope of it. All I could think of was, "Holy shit, I'm totally busted," and right away I started to confess to this lawman. I did not want to go to jail. I was sorry, I was—oh man, I was in one hell of a mess.

The year before I had heard that another boat in our company was under a criminal investigation for the same thing. The two captains of the *Unimak* were facing criminal conspiracy charges and were looking at prison terms. For the time being the charges are being dragged out by the company's entourage of lawyers, and both skippers and the *Unimak* continued to fish. I spent a lot of time talking to these guys about this and they were scared out of their minds. Now I had just joined them.

Never in my life can I remember being so afraid. I had spent two days in a county jail as a college kid for drunk driving and it gave me enough of a taste of what this was all about. I wanted nothing to do with jail ever again.

I confessed to all of Ernie's allegations immediately, thinking it was all off the record at the time. Just man to man, I foolishly thought, when he agreed. I now know there is no such thing as off the record with these people. But I don't blame Ernie. He was doing his job and since then supported me and helped me to come to terms with what was ahead.

Little did I know when I opened my mouth without a company attorney present, I had just written my own ticket to being an ex-fisherman.

* * *

July 2002

On Thursday, July 11, I was four days from finishing up our first summer trip for *B* season. We had a big trip onboard and were fishing in deep water, chasing our allowable bycatch of turbot, black cod, and deepwater red fish—all high dollar money fish. I was in a great mood and the weather was one of those perfect Alaskan summer days. Killer whales were feeding off our discard shoot and humpback whales were feeding on mass schools of herring.

The satellite phone rang about noon and it was the office. An indictment was handed down against the boat and me. It included a fine of $360,000, which was bad enough, but even worse, the boat would lose two six-week periods on its fishing permit the following year. This would mean the equivalent of an additional $2–3 million fine in lost fishing time.

There went my good mood. My knees gave out and I fell in my chair.

"We need you to come down to Seattle after this trip to take care of this," said the company president before hanging up with no further explanation.

I kept the news to myself for the next three days. I didn't sleep and had no idea what to expect. In my wildest dreams, however, I never saw the immensity of the storm that was about to come my way.

A NEW DIRECTION

I walked into the company president's Seattle office for a scheduled appointment at 8 a.m. on August 15, 2002. I waited for forty-five minutes before he finally walked through the door without greeting me, sat down at his desk, and handed me a letter from the company's attorney. The letter was short and sweet. It said the company would be coming after me personally for the fines and lost fishing time, and I needed to get my own attorney. I sat in shock and looked up at him.

"We're letting you go. Get a good lawyer," was all he had to say.

I didn't know what to say. I was terribly sick to my stomach. I stood up and walked out in a daze. I drove back to my motel room, fell into a corner, and cried for I have no idea how long. Thoughts of suicide ran through my head, like a storm unleashed with all its fury. With my soul and mind feeling like they were ripped up in miniature pieces, I lost all control of my emotions. I felt as if all I held dear to me in the fishing world was gone—ripped away.

After a period of time I calmed down enough to call Barb. She was pretty unforgiving, but managed to calm me down somewhat and to put things in perspective. There were two young girls around Dancia's age that were missing in the U.S. at the time from being abducted, and it didn't look good that they would be found alive.

"Those parents would give up their jobs, their homes, and all their worldly possessions to have their daughters back," she said. "Yeah, you screwed up—big time—but you have two beautiful young children who love you and need you. They don't care that you're not a big fishing captain anymore. They'll love it that you're home all the time to play with them."

We talked some more and I told her more details. Barb was pretty fed up that on top of my womanizing I was now coming clean about being a dishonest fisherman to boot, after years of assuring her otherwise. My life as a commercial fisherman was not the only part of my life that was irretrievably damaged. She suggested I go see a movie to try and relax my mind, and tried to assure me that although this was an incredibly difficult time, I would get through it. And that I needed to get through it for the sake of our children.

I hung up with her and called Ernie Soper in Dutch Harbor. In an emotional release of tears and fear, I became a government witness. I did this not to save myself, for I was already lost, but to try and right the wrong.

The next three weeks were hell. I returned to our sailboat at Ko Olina Marina, which was now in a holding pattern in Hawaii. Barb and the kids stayed at a condo we purchased up the road in Makaha, and life returned to some semblance of normalcy as our two children returned to school in late July as part of the extended year school system in Hawaii.

I talked to the Feds, went to doctors for help mentally, and began to deal with the fact Barb was finally following through on a divorce. This last incident was the straw that broke the camel's back. Seven years of me being unfaithful, dishonest, and abusive was a toll no woman should ever have to pay in a marriage. Lying about my entire fishing career was unforgivable to Barb, who was a career biologist before going to work part-time as an environmental specialist for the Federal Emergency Management Agency (FEMA) in 1998.

Barb believed in the system that I tried to shirk. I lied to her that I didn't pre-sort and assured her I fished honestly. We had discussed similar issues through the years, and I had convinced her I was a huge supporter of the NMFS fisheries management program. I even used being married to a former observer as validation to other observers assigned to my boat. On top of all my other problems, my current problems made her lose the remaining threads of respect she may have had for me.

Barb quickly turned into the primary wage earner for herself and the children, and made herself available for work with FEMA. They deployed her to Alaska and I was left to take care of our two children, now three and seven years old, for the next three weeks. In my state of mind I didn't think I could do this. But Barb, in leaving, probably saved my life. I had two young children that needed me and I had to get myself together for their sake.

I took the kids to school, played countless hours with them, took the boat out and fished whenever I could, and attended ongoing anger management classes I had started back in 2001. I reached out to a friend, Chris Leon, who taught the classes and who, until then, I had taken for granted. Chris is a Ph.D. clinical psychologist who helps troubled men who are mostly domestic violence and abusive types. He had always said I could call him any time, 24 hours a day, and I began taking him up on his offer as I struggled to pull my life back together.

Others who I found really cared about me and went way out of their way to call and lend their support included Mark Kandianis, owner of the Kodiak Fish Company, and Richard McLellan, my long-time Alaskan fishing buddy. I originally knew both of them in Maine and, like me, they had each made the move to work in Alaska in the 1980s. During this critical time period in my life, they called me almost every day to offer advice and assured me I would get through this bad time.

* * *

September 7, 2002

With my two children tearing apart my soon-to-be ex-wife's condo while she was off working for FEMA, I felt at peace. I still didn't know how the civil suit against me and Iquique would play out, but I but I knew I couldn't let it consume me.

At 40 years old, I made a pack with myself to change who I would be in the future. It took me 39 years to realize I didn't like who I was, yet I still had the second half of my life to become a different person.

Chris Leon gave me a poem entitled Autobiography in Five Chapters from the Tibetan Book of Living and Dying that I think it is the most beautiful thing I have ever read. It talks about walking down the street and coming across a deep hole in the sidewalk. It uses examples of falling in, pretending you don't see it and still falling in, seeing it but falling in anyway, walking around it, and choosing to walk down a different street. I wrote my own version below. I, too, will walk down another street.

Hard Lessons Learned

1) I see a great school of codfish.
   I set my net and make a tow.
   I hang up on a wreck.
   I am pissed at the world.
   I lose my net.

2) I see a great school of codfish.
   I set my net and make a tow.
   I pretend I don't know there's a wreck in the area.
   I hang up and can't believe I'm in the same place.
   I am mad, but it isn't my fault.
   I free my net.
   My net is toast.

3) I see a great school of codfish.
   I set my net and make a tow.
   I try hauling back before the wreck.
   I snag it anyway—it's a habit.
   My eyes are open and I know where I am.
   It is my fault.
   I catch a few fish in the torn net.

4) I see a great school of codfish.
   I set my net and make a tow.
   I tow around the wreck.
   I am proud of myself.
   I catch a heap of fish.

5) The moral is—I'm a knucklehead who learns the hard way.

* * *

I ended up owning the *Jack of Hearts* until 2006, living on the boat long after Barb and I divorced in 2003. As our divorce was being finalized, we took that boat together from the Hawaiian Islands down through the Line Islands, stopping in Palmyra for a week (the maximum time allowed now that it's managed by the Nature Conservancy) and a month in Fanning Island, before heading on for a month each in American Samoa and Western Samoa before Barb left for good. I thought I could show her I was a changed man, but it didn't work. There was too much water under the bridge.

I continued on to Tonga and other ports before finally sailing to Vanuatu in 2005, where I spent time working as a sport fishing guide for billfish. The old gal put some water under her keel and her tired old Perkins engine had 8,000 hours on it—proof that I never did figure out the sailing part very well.

A new phase of my life had started, and I began to find an even harder way to make an easy living—another story that is yet to be told.

AFTERWORD

The groundfish stocks in the Bering Sea and Gulf of Alaska are very healthy. These are some of the richest waters in the world and they are managed carefully. NMFS has been involved in this fishery from the start and continues to do a wonderful job of managing the stocks. The way they handle bycatch is a different matter.

Modern day factory trawlers are probably the most efficient fishing platforms in the world. They put up some of the best quality seafood and the products are sold throughout the world, including the United States, Europe, and Asia. These huge plants at sea feed millions of people.

In the past few years the groundfish fleet, especially factory trawlers, has come under attack from many different sides that range from Greenpeace to our own Alaskan senators. This is truly a shame because these groups are biased towards this fishery without a fundamental knowledge of what's really going on.

The trawling industry is fighting for its life and faces an uncertain future. There are thousands of men and women who make their living onboard these vessels. It's an industry that supports many businesses and directly influences the economy in Alaska. The people who work on factory trawlers come from varied ethnic backgrounds, including men and women from Mexico, South America, Russia, Poland, Asia, in addition to just about every state. The vessels are huge melting pots and it's amazing how so many different cultures can co-exist in such a confined place. The politicians of the world could learn a great lesson.

Some of the crew stick together on the same boat for years. These guys are blood loyal and are some of the hardest workers of the world. As a captain, I always tried to get to know the names of my crewmembers and to take the time to learn something about each of them. The repeat guys and the loyal core group are the ones I got to know quite well, and I grew extremely fond of some of them.

I had one Vietnam processor in his early twenties named Thom Lee who stayed with me for some time. Thom Lee is one of the proudest people I've ever met. He always had a smile on his face and would do any job asked of him. When the fishing was hot, he would tell me, "Thank you for the fish." When it was slow, he would say, "Don't worry, Captain, we will find them."

Whenever we were having a good trip I'd ask Thom Lee, "What are you going to do with all your money?"

His answer was always the same. "I shall make my family happy," he'd say, and smile with a glow. Thom Lee is a great man and is just one of many.

My former redneck relief skipper, Butch Taylor, has a heart as big as the boat. Mireck, a Polish deck boss turned into a first mate, is an excellent twine man and is the most natural fisherman I've ever known. All my crewmembers were special and the majority of the people I fished with are some of the finest human beings I've ever known.

Corruption in the Alaskan fishing industry has become rampant and I feel strongly that foreigners should not be allowed to fish American waters as they continue to do as fishmasters. Too many Americans are essentially paper skippers onboard, meaning they're the captains on paper only to meet the NMFS legal requirements. In these situations, which are many, the foreigners control the actual fishing and operation of the vessels. Too many American fishermen are currently out of work to let such an atrocity occur. Laws need to be changed and NMFS and the fishermen need to learn how to work together. Trust needs to be built and established mutually between the two groups.

What I did was wrong and I will always feel remorse that I let down all the people I did. I made a huge mistake that I realize I need to take responsibility for, even though I felt forced into the situation because of the pressure placed on me by an uncaring and corrupt company to meet their production numbers. The last joke's on me, as the company failed to follow through on their promise to cover any fines that would be incurred by my fishing methods. Instead, they gave me the boot and made me a scapegoat.

Are all fishermen dishonest? Of course not. But a lot of us bend the rules, break laws we don't agree with, and do what at times we believe needs to be done to make boat payments, money for the crew, and for ourselves. This is not meant to be an excuse. I knew what I was doing every step of the way and I'm now paying the consequences.

Commercial fishing is a way of life. I truly hope it will last for future generations, and for this reason I will do everything I can to help educate not only those involved in the fishing industry, but the general public. There are some bad laws that need to be changed and some house cleaning needs to be done on a number of fronts. But it's not too late to place the fish back in the hands of the traditional American fisherman. With the right management, I believe there's a fighting chance.

As Chris Leon would say, peace.

Read on for an excerpt from

To See a Green Flash
Corky Decker

Available in March 2011

Prologue

York, Maine—March 22, 1949

Twenty lobster traps remained in the string to be retrieved as ice began to form on the rails of the *Sandra J*. Eric was averaging a lobster per pot and wanted to get the last pots hauled and re-baited before the wind, already a stiff thirty knots, kicked up any more. A lobster per trap was good fishing in the winter, and with a northeast blow building, he wasn't sure when he'd be able to make the ten-mile steam out to Boon Island to tend his gear again.

Eric's wife, Sandra, was pregnant with their first child and he really needed the money those remaining lobsters would bring. His mind started to wonder about the baby not quite here, but expected any day. A boy, please let it be a boy, he thought. A son to take fishing. I'll teach him everything about the water. To share his greatest love with, a son was his most precious desire.

Eric never shared these thoughts with Sandra. He would never let her have any doubts that if the child turned out to be a girl he would not love her with all his heart. Eric knew he would treat a daughter like a princess; but still, please let the baby be a boy. My first-born. He grinned foolishly at the thought.

He turned the bow into the wind, bringing the starboard right side of the boat along the first buoy of his last remaining string. As he leaned over the rail to gaff the buoy aboard, a wave crashed into the hull of his wooden boat, blasting a wall of icy water into his face and soaking him despite the oil gear he wore. God, it was cold. Ice formed on contact with the rails in the twenty-degree temperature. He missed the buoy. Damn. He'd have to make another pass. *I should just leave these last pots and head in* he thought angrily, knowing he'd finish up the string.

Swinging the old boat in a tight circle, he lined up for another pass at the buoy. Steadily increasing winds built the seas to over six feet and it was starting to get nasty out. He knew he had to hurry if he was going to haul those last few pots. His temper began to flare for the time wasted on the first failed attempt.

Eric successfully snags the buoy on the second pass and grunts his satisfaction as he places the warp in the davit and takes a couple wraps around the cathead, starting the pot to the surface. As the wooden pot breaks the surface, Eric grabs the bridle and swings the pot onto the rail. Opening the door, his pulse kicks up a few rpms as he sees four nice two-pound males in the parlor inside the lobster pot. Quickly, he pegs the claws, pushing a small wooden peg in the joint of the pincers, and places the lobsters in his holding tank. He re-baits the pot with a bait bag of herring, closes the door, and sends the pot back to the bottom.

He slams the boat into gear and pushes the throttle forward, sending it launching ahead in the heavy seas towards the next buoy in the string. The rough weather causes his boat to pitch and roll more than usual, and the neat coil of thirty fathoms of pot warp at Eric's feet becomes a loose pile of line. As the boat picks up speed, the warp begins flying off the deck.

The boat hits a wave hard, causing Eric to lose his balance. He stumbles into the dash, losing his grip on the wheel. In his struggle to keep balance, his right foot lands in the coil of warp and it immediately begins wrapping tightly around his leg. The boat, at damn near full throttle, is doing seven knots into the swells. Dropping like an anchor, the sixty-pound oak trap attached to the warp heads straight for the ocean floor. Caught in the warp, Eric is slammed hard into the stern transom.

A lobsterman's worst nightmare is getting caught in a warp and dragged overboard. Eric is well aware of what is happening. He keeps a sharp knife in a sheath tied to the stern quarter for just such an emergency. As his lower body starts to be pulled overboard by the extreme pressure of the warp, his strong cotton-gloved hands desperately hold onto the rail. He stares at the bone-handled knife a mere three feet from his head and knows he must reach that knife if he is going to survive. He has precious few seconds to act.

Time slows and each second becomes a still frame during his struggle to reach the knife, like a page turned slowly in a book. With the knife less than a foot from his left hand and with a strength born of desperation, he releases his left hand from the rail and makes an attempt at the knife. The fingers of his right hand are torn free and his body is quickly engulfed by the North Atlantic like a flash of lightning.

The shock of the freezing water steals the breath from his lungs, as he feels himself being pulled down. Eric's last thought is he has failed Sandra and his unborn child. He knows he will never see his baby. Mercifully, darkness comes overtakes him, like a candle blown out by the wind.

The next day the Coast Guard finds the *Sandra J* piled up on the rocks of Boon Island. The same day Eric's son, Benjamin, is born during the worst nor'easter in years.

Chapter 1

"Goddamn wharf rats," Old Man Perkins shouts, shattering the peacefulness of the early summer dawn. "Those little shits stole my punt again," he bellows to no one in particular, and at the same time everyone within earshot.

Hearing the old man, Billy and Ben stop dead in their tracks at the top of the gangway, quickly ducking behind a bait barrel. "I thought you said you returned the punt last night," Ben whispers.

"I lied. It started getting dark and the tide was running strong, so I left it on the other side of the river and walked home," Billy confesses.

"So what did you think, the old man's punt would row itself back to the dock this morning?" asks Ben, holding his head in his hands. "Jeez, we're in deep shit now."

"You're not kidding," a deep booming voice explodes like thunder, as strong massive hands close on the base of the two terrified boys' necks, lifting the ten-year-olds clean into the air.

"Now where's my skiff, goddamn it," the pissed-off old man screams at the boys, his spittle misting their faces like fine rain. His breath smells like old pipe tobacco.

"It's across the river, Mr. Perkins. The tide was running hard and it was getting too dark to make it back last night," Ben said, his voice shaking. We were going to fetch it just now and have it tied up before you noticed it was missing," said Billy, lying as usual.

"We just had to grab an oar from Billy's dad's punt so we each had one. We didn't think you'd be heading out so early," Ben adds quickly, thinking he has to come up with something believable to justify why they were not already busy returning the skiff from across the river.

Old Man Perkins releases his painful grip on the boys' necks and the pair falls in a heap at his feet. He stares at the two boys in silence for what seems like forever. Finally, sighing deeply, his hardened features soften. "Okay, let's go. I have a spare oar in the truck. I'll drop you two off across the river, and you two water rats best paddle your asses off and beat me back here, you hear?"

"Yes sir," they say in unison, as unspoken "boy are we lucky" looks pass between the two. They follow the old man to his battered Ford pickup. The old man looks out and sees Billy's dad's boat is missing from its mooring.

"Missed your dad this morning, I see. I think I'll make you two boys go with me today for the rightful payment of stealing my skiff."

"Tuna fishing or lobstering?" Ben asked.

The old man stops and looks up into the morning sky to the west. "No wind or clouds. Maybe it'll be a day to iron a fish or two. Now hop in the back. I don't want you two jawing me to death on the way over."

The boys run around the back of the truck and pile into the front cab, ignoring the old man. Old Man Perkins climbs into the truck, trying not to grin. Youth. Ah, to be young again, he thinks. These two must have saltwater running though their veins. And look at me, nothing but a soft old man. Here they go and steal my skiff and I reward them for it. He shakes his head, knowing he will enjoy the day as much as the two young boys.

*　*　*

The alarm jolts Ben from his sleep. He rolls over and searches for the off switch in the darkness as the dream of that day seven years ago fades back into the place in his mind where memories are stored. Time to go lobstering—4:45 a.m. His sleep-filled mind brings a yawn that starts deep in his chest. Maybe, just maybe, it'll be a tuna day he thinks with a smile as his eyes snap wide open.